Running
Pool

The Basics

by Steve Bateman

Copyright

Running with Power: The Basics

Wokingham: from1runner2another, 2024
ISBN 978-1-7390906-0-9 (1st Edition)
also available as an eBook

Published in the United Kingdom. Illustrations by the author and from the public domain. All rights reserved, especially the right to copy and distribute, including the translation rights. No part of this book may be reproduced, processed, stored electronically, copied or distributed in any format, print or electronic, without the copyright holder's written permission.

© 2024 by from1runner2another,
Wokingham, United Kingdom.

All trademarks, service marks, and company names are the property of their respective owners.

Disclaimer: This book is for informational and educational purposes. Please consult your healthcare provider or a certified running coach *before* beginning any running program.

- Training 135
  - What's coming up? 135
  - What happens when you train? 139
  - Training Stress Score (TSS) 147
  - Chronic Training Load (CTL) and Acute Training Load (ATL) 150
  - Training Stress Balance (TSB) 155
  - Running Stress Score (RSS) 160
  - Running Stress Balance (RSB) 163
  - Ramp Rate 167
  - Training Intensity Distribution 170
  - Which training metrics should you use? .. 174
  - Planning Training 177
  - Choosing a Training Plan 184
  - Detraining 189
- Chapter 6 193
  - Power-Duration Curve 193
    - What's coming up? 193
    - The relationship between Intensity and Duration 195
    - Power-Duration Curve (PDC) 200
    - Reserve Work Capacity (RWC) 208
    - Riegel Exponent 212
    - Time To Exhaustion (TTE) 217
- Chapter 7 219

- Races & Events 219
  - What's coming up? 219
  - Running Effectiveness (RE) 221
  - Setting event targets 225
  - Tapering 233
  - The event 238
- Chapter 8 245
  - Environments 245
    - What's coming up? 245
    - Heat, Humidity and Altitude 247
    - Treadmills 251
    - Trails & Ultras 257
- Chapter 9 259
  - Frequently Asked Questions (FAQ) 259
    - What's coming up? 259
    - How is power measured when running? . 260
    - How do I use the power numbers? 261
    - Is there a relationship between power and duration? 262
    - What are CP and FTP? 263
    - How can I determine my CP/FTP? 264
    - How do I keep my CP/FTP updated? 265
    - Is my running CP/FTP the same as my cycling or swimming FTP? 266

For Jane

My wife, best friend, editor, and #1 supporter

*How do you always manage to pop-up
just when I need to hear a "whoop whoop"?!*

Contents

Copyright..i

Contents.. v

Is power the next great running metric?.................... 1

Introduction... 7
    Who this book is for.. 7
    How this book is organised 11
    How to use this book.. 13
    My experience with power............................... 15

Chapter 1 19
    Why Run with Power? 19
    The benefits of power.. 19
    What is Running with Power? 25
    How does power compare to other measures of intensity?.......................................31
    What's different about Running with Power?.. 42

Chapter 2 47
    Getting Started 47

What's coming up?	47
You'll need to make some choices	49
The Stryd Ecosystem	56
TrainingPeaks / WKO	60
Choose your own combination	63
Making the connections	73
Is it complicated to start Running with Power?	79

Chapter 3	83
Fundamentals	83
What's coming up?	83
What happens when you exercise?	85
Critical Power (CP)	90
Functional Threshold Power (FTP)	94
Auto-Calculated Critical Power (Auto-CP)	98
Which CP/FTP should you use?	102
Maintaining a valid CP/FTP	107

Chapter 4	113
Workouts	113
What's coming up?	113
Your watch display	116
Height & Weight settings	123
Other watch settings	129
Chapter 5	135

- Training 135
  - What's coming up? 135
  - What happens when you train? 139
  - Training Stress Score (TSS) 147
  - Chronic Training Load (CTL) and Acute Training Load (ATL) 150
  - Training Stress Balance (TSB) 155
  - Running Stress Score (RSS) 160
  - Running Stress Balance (RSB) 163
  - Ramp Rate 167
  - Training Intensity Distribution 170
  - Which training metrics should you use? .. 174
  - Planning Training 177
  - Choosing a Training Plan 184
  - Detraining 189
- Chapter 6 193
  - Power-Duration Curve 193
    - What's coming up? 193
    - The relationship between Intensity and Duration 195
    - Power-Duration Curve (PDC) 200
    - Reserve Work Capacity (RWC) 208
    - Riegel Exponent 212
    - Time To Exhaustion (TTE) 217
- Chapter 7 219

Races & Events 219
What's coming up? 219
Running Effectiveness (RE) 221
Setting event targets 225
Tapering 233
The event 238

Chapter 8 245
Environments 245
What's coming up? 245
Heat, Humidity and Altitude 247
Treadmills 251
Trails & Ultras 257

Chapter 9 259
Frequently Asked Questions (FAQ) 259
What's coming up? 259
How is power measured when running? . 260
How do I use the power numbers? 261
Is there a relationship between power and duration? 262
What are CP and FTP? 263
How can I determine my CP/FTP? 264
How do I keep my CP/FTP updated? .. 265
Is my running CP/FTP the same as my cycling or swimming FTP? 266

- Is CP/FTP the only metric I should monitor? 267
- How do I use power when planning training? 269
- How can I set power-based workout targets? 270
- Can I use power to monitor my training load? 271
- How can I set race/event targets? 273
- Power doesn't tell me what time I might achieve – what does? 274
- Can I Run with Power on a treadmill? 275
- Can I Run with Power on trails or ultras? 276
- How can I keep track of all this "stuff"? 277
- Where can I find power-based training plans? 278
- Where can I find coaches who Coach with Power? 279
- I have more questions ... where can I ask them? 280

Glossary 281

Bibliography 291

Afterwords 315

Is power the next great running metric?

According to Stryd (who sell a footpod power meter), the number of runners uploading power data from the World Marathon Majors has doubled every year since 2016.

All the major running watch manufacturers (Garmin, Coros, Polar, Suunto, and even Apple) have added wrist-based power to their new models.

And the membership of Facebook groups focused on Running with Power has exploded in the last few years.

Is Running with Power a magic bullet? Or a passing fad?

Running with Power is neither.

As with any challenging pursuit, your running won't always go well.

But Running with Power is an approach that gives *you* the greatest chance of achieving *your* best performance while minimising injury risk.

Elite runners can benefit from training and racing with power ...

If you're trying to qualify for the US Olympic Trials, the last thing you want is for a tunnel to scramble your GPS data, but that's precisely what happened to Nicole Lane in the opening mile of 2019's Chicago marathon. It didn't matter; she was Running with Power using a Stryd footpod, and didn't need accurate GPS or pace data. Her training had enabled her coach, Steve Palladino, to calculate a personalised event target that would give her the best result she was capable of. Nicole ran to her power target and finished almost three minutes ahead of the qualifying time.

Power enables you to *quantify the effort* with which you're running – effort is what the body feels.

It allows you to identify the individualised effort *beyond which you'll fatigue much more quickly* – something previously needing lab-based testing to identify.

It enables you to identify, based on your current fitness, the effort you can *maintain for a specific event* – rather than running to a goal time that may or may not be achievable.

You don't need to be Olympic standard to benefit from Running with Power ...

Here's Ewan's story: "I ran and raced a lot as a kid until the age of 18. That would be the last chunk of consistent running until 17 years later ... fast forward to age 35, my then girlfriend (and now wife) got fed up with me banging on about being a decent runner as a kid and signed me up to the Edinburgh marathon. I ran 3:26, got hooked and then spent five years getting down to 2:19 aged 40 (3 years ago now). I used Stryd once I started taking on more of my own coaching to manage my training load and training zones. It helped me hone my marathon racing and pacing approaches ... over time, I've become less dependent on it, with RPE playing more of a role."

Power means you can target training more precisely than pace or heart rate so that you can *stimulate the specific adaptations* you need for your upcoming event.

Power uses your completed workouts to calculate your training load and mix of training intensities, *reducing your risk of over-training* and enabling *tapering that delivers you fresh-legged* to the start line.

Over time, power can help you to *develop your feel* for how much effort you're putting into your running – your Rate of Perceived Exertion (RPE).

Or, in the words of Charles Howe "power calibrates perceived exertion, perceived exertion modulates power".

You don't even need to be a sub-3-hour marathoner ...

Here's my story: "I started running at 50 and struggled for three years to break 4 hours for the marathon. After training with power for a year, I achieved 1:37 half marathon and 3:49 marathon

PBs – without injury (remarkably for my age), and with runs that were challenging, but that progressed without me feeling the progression – runs that felt relaxed and in control."

Power works for anyone willing to *train based on effort*.

It gives you *real-time feedback* about how hard you're running – *feedback that is personal to you* and applies whether you're running fast, slow, uphill, downhill, or for shorter or longer durations.

It *can be used by anyone* regardless of age or running experience.

You don't need to be running marathons or half marathons …

The Stryd website tells the story of Anna P, a 42-year-old who wanted to run 5k in under 30 minutes [*Stryd: Training for Your 5K Personal Best*].

She completed a couch to 5k plan and finished her first 5k in 31:37. Her new target was to beat 30 minutes, but she was stuck – after seeing weekly improvements, she'd stopped improving. A friend recommended a Stryd footpod. Her response? "Are you crazy? That's for you because you run marathons. That's not for a snail like me." But she tried it and used a Stryd training plan with a mix of easy and harder workouts; she ran her second 5k in 27:38, an improvement of 4 minutes!

Is it a magic bullet? A passing fad?

It's worth repeating: your running won't always go well, but Running with Power gives *you* the greatest chance of achieving *your* best performance while minimising injury risk.

Why wouldn't you want that?

Introduction

Who this book is for

This book is for runners who want to understand Running with Power. By that, I don't mean running with a powerful stride or looking powerful when you run. I mean using power to gauge the effort with which you run – your running **intensity**.

Some assumptions

If you're reading this book, I assume you're a runner who's interested in or already Running with Power.

I assume you want to understand how to use Running with Power to improve your running.

And I assume that you run races or events and that your training includes higher intensity workouts – that you're not just running for fun.

Given the above, you probably fall into one of the following categories:

1. Exploring – you're deciding if Running with Power could benefit you.

2. Beginner – you've decided to try Running with Power, and you want to understand how to use the metrics and models.

3. Experienced – you already Run with Power and are familiar with the metrics and models but want to deepen your understanding.

If so, this book is for you.

Finally, I assume you're happy to collect and review data about your running. Most data collection can be automated, with sophisticated running watches and even more sophisticated websites and tools that can crunch the data and show you conclusions. But it's worth noting that to get the most out of Running with Power, you *will* need to collect and review your workout data … or you'll need to hire a coach who can do that for you.

One thing I don't assume …

I don't assume you're using a particular running watch or power meter, and I don't assume you'll use specific apps to plan or review your training. This book is about Running with Power. Whether you use wrist-based Garmin power and TrainingPeaks, an Apple Watch with a Stryd footpod and the Stryd PowerCenter, or any other combination of equipment and apps, the metrics and models are the same – this book focuses on those.

Some clarifications

There are some things that this book doesn't do. It doesn't:

- Provide training plans. If you're looking for power-based training plans, you can find them on the web (see the **Frequently Asked Questions (FAQ)** chapter for links to training plans).

- Dive deep into research. The models are based on research, and there is ongoing research into Running with Power, but this book doesn't explore that research. Instead, it provides a detailed **Bibliography** so you can read the research yourself (if you're interested).

- Tell you what to do. The book explores Running with Power models and describes how those models can be applied to your running. If there is more than one model you could use, the book describes the different options and why you might choose one over another to make the choice that's right for you. And if that's not enough, there are active Facebook groups where you can ask questions or search to see if the question's been asked before (see the **Frequently Asked Questions (FAQ)** chapter for links to Facebook groups).

- Offer personalised coaching. This book certainly can't do that, but a growing group of coaches can offer personalised, power-based coaching (see the **Frequently Asked Questions (FAQ)** chapter for links to coaches).

Is this book for you?

If you're looking for a practical, experience-based guide to Running with Power, this book can be that guide.

It's based on my own experience of Running with Power and coaching others to Run with Power.

And it's informed by many, many discussions about Running with Power that have taken place in Facebook groups.

How this book is organised

Here's a brief overview of the contents of this book.

We begin with the key question **Why Run with Power?** including a definition of power, information about the benefits of Running with Power and a comparison of power to other measures of running intensity – pace, heart rate, and perceived exertion.

Getting Started provides some guidance on equipment and supporting apps, the choices you need to make, and how you can choose how to use power in your running.

Fundamentals covers Critical Power and Functional Threshold Power. It dips briefly into the underlying physiology (for context), then covers these fundamental metrics that underpin almost every metric used when Running with Power.

Workouts contains information that will help you get the most out of power when running and that will ensure your workouts provide accurate data to calculate meaningful metrics.

Training covers metrics you can use to extract insights from your training and to reduce the risk of injury. It also summarises what's different about using a power-based approach when planning your training schedule and planning individual workouts.

Your Power-Duration Curve brings together content from earlier chapters to show how your workout data builds a complete picture of your individual running ability. It also introduces key metrics used when planning races & events.

Races & Events shows how you can use your Power-Duration metrics to ensure you achieve your best result.

Environments covers Running with Power in different environments – on a treadmill, when trail or ultra running, at different altitudes, or in hot/humid weather. It covers the adjustments that you may choose to (or need to) make.

Frequently Asked Questions (FAQ) contains the questions most frequently asked by runners new to power. Use the FAQ to get a quick overview of Running with Power or a reminder about a specific topic. The answers reference the relevant chapters if you want to explore a question in more detail.

The book finishes with a **Glossary** and a detailed **Bibliography** that you can use for further reading or research.

How to use this book

This book was written to be versatile. If you're new to Running with Power, you can read it from cover to cover – later content builds on earlier content. If you're familiar with Running with Power, you can skip topics or dip into specific topics of interest. Either of these approaches will help you become familiar with the content so you can refer to it later when you need to refresh your memory or remind yourself about a specific topic.

After you've become familiar with the book, you may find yourself taking advantage of its *just-in-time* features: a clear and consistent topic structure; "what's coming up" at the start of each chapter and a summary at the start of each section; icons highlighting key information ★ and advice ☺; a Frequently Asked Questions chapter; a glossary of terms and definitions, with links to relevant content within the book; a complete bibliography with links to webpages and books for more information.

Unfortunately, the *just-in-time* features also mean that this book repeats things!

This isn't an attempt to increase the size of the book. Instead, it ensures that *all* the relevant information is in each section, which means that if you dip into a specific section, you won't need to refer to other sections or drop back a few pages to fully understand what you're reading.

Use the book as a practical guide

Do what works for you.

The book was written to be a practical guide and an interesting read, not one of those dusty, dry volumes left on the bookshelf.

If you have the paperback version, scribble notes in the margin and add sticky notes on pages you want to keep track of. If you have the eBook version, add your own notes or use X-Ray (for Kindle).

There's nothing I'd like better than to meet runners or running coaches who found the book so valuable that they have a grubby, well-thumbed copy in their back pocket or kit bag.

A note about style

I'm British, and the book is written in British English, so there may be a few spellings or phrases that are, well … British. I make no apologies for these, and if you use another variant of English, I hope you enjoy the trip.

[italics in square brackets] refer to items in the bibliography at the end of the book. If you're reading an electronic version of the book, you should be able to click the *[item]* to go to the bibliography; if you have the paperback, the bibliography is organised alphabetically.

My experience with power

I've been Running with Power since 2018.

I never set out to Run with Power. In fact, I never set out to be a runner.

I was a squash player. Every Sunday, against a few friends. We weren't particularly good, but it was a good workout with some beers and conversation afterwards.

Then I turned 50, and squash was getting harder to play. I started running, thinking that running would help me stay fit enough to play squash.

Eventually, squash became too much, but by that time, I was hooked on running. I'd set and then improved a few Personal Bests (PBs) and ran my first marathon in 2015. The training went well (I thought), but the marathon didn't – I ended up walking most of the second half.

This continued for my next four marathons, despite trying different training plans based on training by heart rate or training by pace. The workouts made sense, but it was difficult to hit the targets, especially in sunny or humid conditions, when it was windy, or when running uphill or downhill. I was never sure I'd completed the training as the author intended, and the prescriptions in the plans didn't seem very precise. For example: "run at 5-10 seconds slower than a 10k pace". Not knowing my 10k pace, I used online calculators with pace calculations that relied on population averages across hundreds of runners, and I was never sure I was running at the correct pace.

I can't remember how I discovered the Stryd power meter. But having found it, it seemed a much better way to train – based on *my physiology*, running to intensities (or effort levels) that were specific to *my ability* and allowing fine control of *my training and racing targets*.

Training using a power meter isn't new and is not specific to running. Cyclists have been training with power since the 1990s, and there's a wealth of knowledge and research into using power meters in cycling, much of which can be applied to using power meters in running.

Looking around for a power-based training plan, I discovered Steve Palladino, a power-based coach and a 2:16 marathoner with 13 years of experience training and racing with cycling power. Steve was on a mission to use power meters to make a significant step forward in running, just as power meters already had for cycling.

I bought his marathon plan in mid-2018, trained with power through the autumn and in late 2018, set a half-marathon PB of 1:36:55. I continued the power-based training through the following spring and set a marathon PB of 3:49:24. I'm not a fast runner, but I'm passionate about running and how to get the most from my training and the events I enter.

I joined Steve Palladino's Facebook group *[Palladino; PPP Facebook group]* and started reading his Running with Power article library [*Palladino; Article library*], which came complete with power-based calculators to calculate my Critical Power and calculators to set race goals.

With few calculators available for Running with Power, I collaborated with Steve and Alex Tran to consolidate Steve's calculators into a single calculator – SuperPower Calculator for Sheets [*SPC for Sheets*]; later, we collaborated with Mikael Lönn to create SuperPower Calculator for the Web [*SPC for Web*].

My fascination with power has continued, and when I qualified as a running coach in 2021, I started a coaching practice using Running with Power and have since applied power-based principles to coaching using critical speed. I've also written numerous short guides about Running with Power: using a Garmin; on a treadmill; Running with Power in 10 minutes. All of which has led to this book and the hope of reaching many more runners.

★ I'd recommend Running with Power to anyone who wants to use a science-backed, metrics-based, individualised approach to training and racing.

Chapter 1

Why Run with Power?

The benefits of power

What's in this section?

Power will enable you to determine the race-day target that will produce the best result *based on your fitness*, rather than going into a race or event hoping your goal time is achievable. And it will enable you to run the race *at an effort level you can maintain throughout.*

Power provides *personal training targets matched to your current fitness* to maximise training gains while minimising the risk of injury or over-training.

Power enables you to identify the threshold above which *you* begin to fatigue more quickly so that you can set workout targets *aligned to your ability* rather than guessing at the right intensity or using online calculators based on population averages over hundreds of runners.

Power enables you to maintain *effort-based workout targets* – even in hilly, windy or other environmental conditions.

Power allows you to *monitor the effectiveness of form changes or supplemental work* in a way that isn't possible without power.

Goal-time blues

Have you ever found yourself on the start line with a specific goal time in mind and hoping you can achieve it? "I'd like to run a marathon in under 4 hours" or "I'm aiming for a 50-minute 10k".

Have you ever started an event and been carried away with how good you feel or how fresh your legs are? Before you know it, you're keeping up with the faster runners and unintentionally setting new personal bests for the first parts of a much longer event. As a result, the second half of the event is really tough on tired legs.

Wouldn't it be good to know exactly how much effort you could put into the event right from the start? An effort that you were confident you'd be able to maintain based on your training and current fitness?

★ Power will enable you to determine the race-day power target (effort) that will produce the best result *based on your fitness*, rather than going into a race or event hoping your goal time is achievable. And it will enable you to run the race *at an effort you can maintain throughout*.

Fine-tune your workout targets

How do you know that you're running your "easy" runs easy? Or that your "threshold" runs are actually at the appropriate threshold? How can you be sure a workout "trained" your VO2max?

If you train by heart rate, you may have used a formula to arrive at your maximum heart rate (MHR) or a stress test finishing with an all-out sprint to reach your MHR. And then, for training purposes, you've used your maximum heart rate to determine zones – for example, Zone 2 (for easy runs) might be 70-80% of MHR.

If you train by pace, you may have run all-out 5k or 10k events and used your finish time with an online calculator (e.g. *[Jack Daniels; VDOT]*) to get pace values for different workout types.

I've done that.

But there are issues with these methods:

- They use population averages (averages across hundreds of runners) rather than being specific to you and your current ability.

- They result in zones or target paces that are pretty wide and may not align with your metabolism. When you think you're training "easy", you may be running at too low or too high an intensity.

And if you train at intensities that are wrong for you, either you'll be leaving some training gains unrealised (if your intensities are too low), or you'll increase your risk of injury (if your intensities are too high)

Wouldn't it be better to base your training on *your fitness* at that point in your training plan?

★ Power provides *personal training targets matched to your current fitness* to maximise training gains while minimising the risk of injury or over-training.

Personal power

You may have heard of "threshold runs" or "tempo runs" and how they are one of the most productive training runs that runners can do. They're usually prescribed as interval workouts: "after a warm-up, run 3x 10 minutes at 10k pace with 3 minutes jogging recoveries".

The difficulty with these runs is determining how hard to run them – too high an intensity, and you will fatigue too quickly; too low, and you won't get the full benefit from the workout.

★ Power enables you to identify the threshold above which *you* begin to fatigue more quickly so that you can set workout targets *aligned to your ability* rather than guessing at the right intensity or using online calculators based on population averages over hundreds of runners.

How much effort?

If you're using heart rate as your measure of intensity, there's an additional difficulty – there's usually a delay (a "lag") between changing your running intensity and seeing the change reflected in your heart rate, which makes it challenging to monitor and target heart rate targets during interval workouts.

Over longer runs, you may find that your heart rate steadily increases in response to the effort and in response to increasing fatigue later in the run – your heart rate "drifts".

Power meters reflect real-time changes in effort – there's no lag. And they measure the actual effort you're working at – there's no drift.

If you're using pace as your measure of intensity, there's a different difficulty – unless you're running the workout on the flat, you'll have to run up or down hills: run uphill, and you'll need to increase effort to maintain pace; run downhill, and you'll have to reduce effort. But your body doesn't feel pace; it feels effort. By maintaining your pace and changing your effort, you'll be training at the wrong intensity, and if you maintain your effort, you won't be running to your pace targets.

Some runners use "grade-adjusted pace" or "normalised graded pace" to account for hills, but there aren't many running watches or mobile apps that can display the adjusted pace when running. There are similar issues when running in windy conditions.

★ Power enables you to maintain *effort-based workout targets* – even in hilly, windy, or other environmental conditions.

Running more Effectively

Many runners want to improve how they run – to become better runners. They work on their form or physiology using drills, plyometrics, weight training, hill runs or other supplementary work. But it can be challenging to measure the impact this has.

Running Effectiveness measures how effectively you convert power to speed (your speed:power ratio). It's covered in detail in the **Races & Events** chapter.

Running Effectiveness (and changes in RE over time) can be used to monitor the impact of supplemental work. If effective, your RE for a given speed should increase as you become better at converting power into speed.

Some power meters also offer metrics that can be used to measure improvements in your leg spring (the elastic recoil that stores then releases energy with each stride) and improvements in your horizontal power ratio (how much of the power you're generating is being used to move you forward).

★ Power allows you to *monitor the effectiveness of form changes or supplemental work* in a way that isn't possible without power.

What is Running with Power?

What's in this section?

Power is a measure of how hard you're running, which results from the energy (or effort) you're putting into your run.

A power meter models your running movements to produce a power measurement.

Power measurements reflect your running **intensity** (how hard?) and are combined with time (rather than distance) to measure **duration** (how long?)

Running with Power uses power-duration to plan, execute and monitor your training.

Running with Power is for everyone *unless* you're running purely for health with no races, no higher intensity training … just running for fun

What is power?

Power is measured in Watts and is "the amount of energy transferred or converted per unit time" [*Wikipedia; Power (Physics)*]

In sports, power is a modelled measure of the effort required to run, ride, swim, etc.

When running, it takes more effort to run faster, to run uphill, or to run into a headwind. If you run slower, downhill, or with a tailwind, it takes less effort.

In other words, higher effort = higher modelled power.

How is power measured?

A power meter measures your movements and the forces needed to produce those movements. It models how much energy it took to produce those forces, showing the result in Watts (or optionally in Watts/kg).

★ Power meter readings aren't an exact measurement of the power required to run. Depending on where the power meter is placed, there are many other movements that the meter won't be able to measure, and there are many internal metabolic processes that a power meter can't measure.

However, the modelled numbers are good enough to be used to Run with Power.

What does power measure?

Whenever you run (or walk, swim, cycle, etc.), that movement can be measured using two pieces of information: How hard? How long?

OK, there are many more ways to measure movement, but let's focus on those two for now.

How hard?

The **intensity** of the movement. Runners use four measurements:

- Heart Rate: higher intensity = faster heart rate (measured in beats per minute / BPM)
- Pace: higher intensity = faster pace (measured in min/km or min/mile)
- Perceived Exertion: higher intensity = higher perceived exertion (measured using a Borg scale)
- Power: higher intensity = higher power (measured in Watts or Watts/kg)

How long?

The **duration** of the movement. Runners use two measurements:

- Distance: longer duration = longer distance (measured in metres/kilometres or yards/miles)
- Time: longer duration = longer time (measured in seconds, minutes, hours or days!)

Runners who want to measure their running can (and do) use any combination of **intensity** and **duration**. Later in this chapter, the different measures are compared, highlighting the strengths and weaknesses of each.

★ For now, it's enough to note that Running with Power uses Power and Time to measure your runs (more frequently referred to as power-duration).

How do you Run with Power?

A power meter or a running watch (or mobile phone) will show you second-by-second power readings as you run, recording the information into a workout file.

You can use these power readings:

- when running – to complete a workout at specific target intensities or within target ranges

- after your run – to review your workout and to adjust your upcoming workouts

- when following a training plan – to monitor training load and training intensity distribution

- when taking part in an event – to target how hard to run the event and to monitor that you're running to target

Will Running with Power be useful for me?

Whether power would be useful for you depends on what you want to achieve with each run rather than on your running ability or the kinds of events you run.

For example:

If you ...	Useful?
are running an event	useful
are running intervals	useful
want to include your run in your training load	useful
are out for a social run, chatting with friends	not useful
have just started running and you're building distance or aerobic volume	not useful

☺ The question of usefulness is really about the situations in which measuring *intensity* is useful, and the above list leads to a conclusion summarised by Steve Palladino in a Facebook post, who'd advise a runner "not to bother with power if they were running purely for health with no races, no higher intensity training ... just aerobic running".

★ There are times when measuring intensity is not useful (and may actually detract from the experience). The rest of the time, measuring intensity and running to specific intensities *is* useful.

As to whether power is the best measure of intensity, that's next.

How does power compare to other measures of intensity?

What's in this section?

Power (your effort) is a measure of intensity, as are heart rate, pace (your speed) and perceived exertion (your feeling of effort).

The four different measures are related. Power measures the effort you're putting into your run. Pace measures the result of translating that effort into forward movement. Heart Rate measures the impact that your effort is having on your cardio-vascular system (to get oxygen to your working muscles). Perceived exertion measures how hard your effort "feels".

However:

- Heart Rate "lags" behind changes to your effort levels, it can "drift" on longer runs, it won't go above your maximum heart rate (even if your effort does) and it can be affected by age, illness, stress, lack of sleep, fatigue, adrenaline, stimulants, humidity, heat, cold and hydration (to name a few!).

- Pace is affected by hills and windy conditions and while pace can be "normalised" to take account of hills, few running watches can do this while you're running. When running an event, it's also very easy to aim for a goal time that's not based on your current fitness (leading to bonking, hitting the wall, and a less enjoyable latter part of longer events).

- Perceived Exertion can be impacted by stress, tiredness, heat, hydration, and other things, making it hard to assess your effort level accurately. In addition, it takes time and training to develop a good feel for perceived exertion, making it impractical for most recreational runners.

- Power is still new to the running community. There are few universal standards and a lot of variation in how different aspects of Running with Power have been implemented. Plus, you will need a power meter or a newer running watch with wrist-based power (see **Getting Started** for some options). But by measuring your effort, power solves a lot of the issues encountered with heart rate, pace, and perceived exertion, and it enables you to fine-tune your training targets and to set achievable race-day goals.

Heart Rate (HR)

Heart rate is easy to measure – stick your fingers on your wrist and count. Increase your intensity, and your heart rate will increase; decrease your intensity and your heart rate will decrease.

But …

Heart rate is a response to your effort, but it's not an immediate change – there may be a few seconds delay (or "lag") before the change is apparent. Which makes heart rate less useful if you're running intervals.

Heart rate can also "drift" during long workouts, so that for the same effort level, it may be higher at the end of a run than at the beginning. Which makes heart rate less useful for longer runs.

Heart rate won't go above your maximum heart rate, even if your effort is much higher – heart rate doesn't cover the complete range of intensities. Which makes heart rate less useful for sprints, hill runs or other higher-intensity workouts.

It can be difficult to target the correct heart rate when trying to "stay in zone 2", and it's possible to find yourself walking just to keep your heart rate in the right zone.

And heart rate can be affected by age, illness, stress, lack of sleep, fatigue, adrenaline, stimulants, humidity, heat, cold and hydration – all things not directly related to your effort. Which makes heart rate less useful in a wide variety of situations.

Pace

Pace is also easy to measure – if you know the distance you ran and how long it took, you can calculate your speed, and speed is the inverse of pace (e.g. 10 kilometres per hour means you'll complete one kilometre every 6 minutes on average – your pace is 6 minutes/km).

But ...

Pace results from your effort (and how effectively you convert that effort into forward motion). As you increase your effort, you increase your pace.

Until you run uphill and find that either you have to increase your effort to maintain the same pace or you have to maintain your effort by letting your pace decrease. The reverse is true when running downhill. Which makes pace less useful when running hilly routes.

If you're running on a windy day, your pace is impacted when you run into a headwind – your effort increases or your pace decreases. The reverse is true when running with a tailwind. Which makes pace less useful when running in windy conditions.

Pace is an external result that may not match the effort required to produce it. This means that it's tough to use pace as a race or event target matched to your current fitness. Your training may have given you a feel for the correct pace to run at, but once on the course, any hills or wind will impact your ability to maintain your pace. Which makes pace less useful when trying to run to a target.

But if you want to achieve a specific time for an event, don't you have to run using pace?

You do, but the real question is whether your goal time (and therefore your pace target) is realistic and reflects your current fitness. If your goal time is unrealistic, you'll be running at a pace you can't sustain. This makes pace less useful when running to an event target *unless* you can be certain that you can maintain that pace (with hills, wind, heat, and other factors).

Rating of Perceived Exertion (RPE)

Rating of Perceived Exertion measures how your effort "feels". Run harder, and it feels harder; run easier, it feels easier.

But ...

Run the same effort when feeling fresh and it will feel different than running it when you feel tired, or hot. Your perceived effort can be impacted by stress, tiredness, heat, hydration, and other things, making it hard to assess your effort level accurately. Which makes perceived effort less useful as an objective measure of intensity.

And it takes time and training to develop a good feel for perceived exertion. Which makes it impractical for the majority of recreational runners.

Power

Power meters show real-time changes. Change how hard you're running, and your power number will change immediately. In fact, if you measure real-time power, you'll find that your power number is constantly changing – many runners use 3-second or 10-second average power to "smooth" the spiky real-time power. It isn't real-time, but it's as close to real-time as you'll need for most situations.

Power won't drift during longer workouts. If your power number steadily decreases throughout a longer run, it's because you're producing less power as you fatigue. In other words, the change in your power number shows you how quickly you're fatiguing – compared to your heart rate, which often *increases* towards the end of longer runs.

There is no maximum power number that a power meter can measure, unlike maximum heart rate. Run faster, and you'll get a higher power number. Run uphill, and you'll get a power number that's higher again. Sprint uphill (!), and you'll get an even higher power number. Your power number is limited only by how much effort you can generate – there is no upper limit, unlike your heart rate.

Your power number can be affected by age, illness, stress, lack of sleep, fatigue, adrenaline, stimulants, humidity, heat, cold and hydration. But that's because your body is affected by those things, impacting the effort you can generate. By measuring your effort, your power number shows you the impact of those things on your running.

If you run uphill (maintaining the same pace), your power number will increase – running at a certain speed uphill takes more effort compared to running on the flat. If you maintain the same effort uphill, your pace will decrease as some of your effort goes into moving you uphill, leaving less to move you forward. The change in your power number reflects how your effort changes – higher effort gives a higher power number, unlike pace, which reduces as effort increases. And you don't need any "normalising" or "adjusting" to maintain a target, as a power target is effort-based.

If you run into a headwind or with a tailwind, your power reflects how your effort changes, like running uphill or downhill.

Unlike pace, power is not an external result that may not match the metabolic effort required to produce it. Power models your effort, producing a power number that represents your metabolic effort.

You can set a target power level or an event based on your current fitness (using power results from your training). Unlike pace, you can maintain your target effort unchanged over hills and through wind. You can even adjust your target power for temperature, humidity, or altitude differences. This means that if you do your race prep correctly, you can run to a target that matches your current fitness and the event conditions – a target that will give you the best result for your current fitness in the event conditions.

Power is an *objective* number based on the effort you're putting into your running. Perceived exertion is a *subjective* assessment (made by the "supercomputer" in your head) that, unless you've had years of training and racing, is less likely to reflect your actual effort.

Are there any downsides to power?

Power is new and unfamiliar to many runners. Learning the models and applying them to your running takes time. But with a little time invested (and this book), you can learn and apply the models.

Most non-runners aren't familiar with power and will ask you about what distance you ran, your target time for your next race, or what time you achieved and whether it was a personal best. That's fine. Talk about times and distances, knowing that your power-based training will allow you to target and measure your training based on effort and that you can use results from your training to plan and run your event, giving you the best possible result based on your actual fitness at the time of the event.

To Run with Power, you need a power meter, which may be an extra expense. But there is a lot of choice including: a footpod that you connect to your watch; wrist-based power built into many newer sports watches; apps or add-ons that you can install on a sports watch that connect to heart rate or running dynamics accessories to produce a power number. These are just some of the options, and they don't have to be expensive (see **Getting Started** for more options).

Power is new to many hardware and website providers catering to runners. As such, there are no universal standards, and there are variations in how different aspects of Running with Power have been implemented. With a few careful choices, it's possible to have a system that, with minimum effort, gives you the information you need to get the most from Running with Power.

Is it only about the numbers?

No, it's not.

Training is, and should be, much more than actions driven by numbers.

When planning training, you should consider your training goals, your specifics (age, ability, injury history, etc.), your supplemental training (strength and mobility work) and other activities that you undertake while training (like cycling, swimming, yoga, or pilates). When executing the plan, you should consider your sleep, nutrition, hydration, your work or family commitments and probably many more things than I can list, most of which you won't be able to measure.

★ But your training should be underpinned by quantitative data – numbers. Power numbers are reliable, repeatable, and valid and can be used to plan and monitor your training progression, as well as enabling you to execute workouts targeting specific intensity levels and durations.

Because power can do so much, you may be tempted to think that your power numbers are *the truth* – by using them to make every training decision, you'll get the best result. But power meters can't measure everything that's happening as you run; for that reason, your power numbers are a guide to the effort you're producing – they're a very good guide, but they are only a guide, not the truth.

★ Rather than *Running by Power* (treating your power numbers as the truth and using them to make every decision), you should be *Running with Power* (using your power numbers as a guide complementing and underpinning other training considerations).

☺ Use all the available data – don't just use your power numbers, but don't ignore them either.

What's different about Running with Power?

What's in this section?

This section describes the experience of Running with Power by comparing what's different when Running with Power to what stays the same.

What stays the same?

You'll still lace up your running shoes and go running.

You'll still follow a training plan if you're training for an event.

Your training plan will still include a mix of workouts – some longer and slower, some shorter and faster (intervals).

If your plan is good and you follow it consistently, your body will still adapt to the training.

And if you already analyse your workouts to track improvements, you'll still analyse your workouts.

What's a little different?

When you lace up your running shoes, you'll also check that your watch and power meter are charged. If you travel with your running kit, you'll also need to take your watch and power meter (and chargers).

If you're training for an event, you'll use a power-based plan, with targets expressed in Watts relative to your CP/FTP. Your CP/FTP represents your current metabolic fitness, which is covered in detail in the **Fundamentals** chapter.

Your training plan will have a mix of workouts, but the workouts may have more focused target ranges. For example, your easy runs may have a maximum intensity of 80% CP/FTP. And your interval runs may have targets of 98-100% or 100-102% of CP/FTP.

Your body will adapt if your plan is good and you follow it consistently. You'll track your improvements using metrics calculated from your completed workouts.

You'll still analyse your workouts but using a different, broader range of metrics.

What's very different?

If you were running by distance previously, you'll switch to running by duration – power-based plans tend to set targets using power-duration values.

★ You'll need to determine your CP/FTP and ensure you monitor it as you train. This will mean running maximum efforts, or CP tests every 4-6 weeks. These maximum efforts or tests should be built into your training plan, but they don't mean you have to miss a training session – because they're maximum efforts, they contribute to your training. Or, in the words of Andrew Coggan, PhD "testing is training too".

★ All of your metrics and your training targets will be based on your current fitness rather than on population averages that may not be appropriate for you as an individual. As your fitness increases (as your CP/FTP improves), your training targets will increase to match – a natural training progression.

You can still run with friends, but *training* with friends will be more challenging. If you train with friends and are used to running intervals together at the same target pace, you may find it harder to do that. Firstly, your friends may not be training with power, so they'll run to pace or HR while you run to power. Secondly, even if they're also running to power and you're all using the same workout targets, it's unlikely that you'll all have the same CP/FTP and that you'll all have the same Running Effectiveness, which means that you'll end up running at different speeds. You can train with your friends, but you will probably find you're not running alongside your friends.

If your training involves hills, you won't need to adjust your targets on the hills. Power measures effort, and you'll maintain that effort over the hills, slowing down on uphills and speeding up on downhills.

★ When you run races or events, you'll run to a power target – you won't run to a goal time. Power targets are based on your current fitness and are much better aligned with what you can achieve compared to a goal time that may be based on wishful thinking. This is probably the most significant difference, and if you've been used to using goal times, running an event without aiming at a specific finish time can be very disconcerting.

That isn't to say that you won't have a goal time in mind (most runners do), but that goal time shouldn't determine the speed at which you run the event. Your speed should be determined by the effort you can maintain for the duration of the event (your fitness), how you convert that effort into speed (your effectiveness), and what happens on the day. Run to your power target, and the rest will follow.

Running to power targets *also* means you won't be able to run with pacers. Pacers aim to finish in a specific time – your finish time depends on your fitness, effectiveness and race-day execution.

Chapter 2

Getting Started

What's coming up?

One thing is true for any unfamiliar subject – we have to start somewhere.

Here's a summary of what the chapter covers ...

To Run with Power, you'll need equipment. You'll also need applications (apps) to plan your power-based workouts and to review and analyse your results.

There are many choices, and a decision for one almost always has implications for the others, making it challenging to balance the alternatives.

This chapter covers how to choose equipment and apps that work together so that you can focus on your training and minimise manual effort.

When choosing, you can go for a ready-made solution, or you can choose your own combination.

One ready-made solution is the Stryd ecosystem, based around the Stryd footpod. Another ready-made solution is TrainingPeaks and WKO.

You can choose your own combination if you don't want to use a ready-made solution. This chapter covers the five steps involved in every workout and presents criteria for evaluating apps and equipment that support these steps. It also lists some better-known apps to evaluate when choosing your combination.

Connecting your apps is essential to avoid manual effort when planning, executing, and reviewing your workouts. This chapter outlines the connections needed for some example setups.

The final section offers a series of setups, starting with the most straightforward and increasing in complexity (and flexibility) in case you're feeling confused or intimidated by all these choices.

You'll need to make some choices

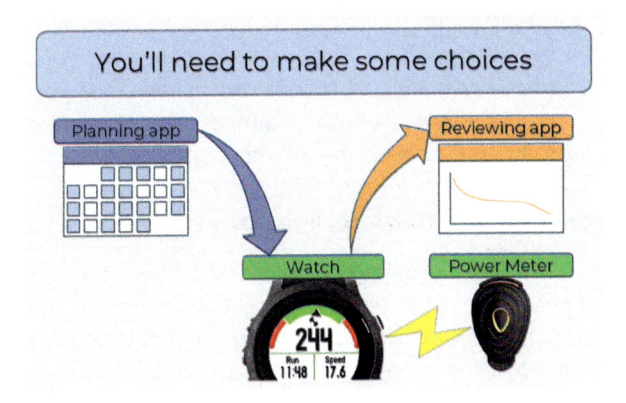

What choices do you need to make?

As with anything new, there are some choices you'll need to make and possibly some things you'll need to buy or subscribe to, depending on what you already use with your running.

To Run with Power, you'll need some equipment:

- A power meter to calculate power numbers.
- A watch that can display the power numbers and record those numbers into a workout file (I'll use the word "watch" to include both watches and phones).

You'll also need some apps (I'll use the word "apps" to include PC/Mac software, as well as web-based and mobile apps):

- A planning app – somewhere to plan your training schedule and individual workouts.
- A reviewing app – somewhere to review your workout results and power metrics so that you can monitor your training and make adjustments based on the results.

What equipment choices are there?

NOTE: The following information was correct when this book was published but may now be outdated, given the speed with which Running with Power is evolving. If you have any questions about whether the following is accurate, please ask in the [flr2a; Facebook Group].

To Run with Power, you'll need a power meter to measure your effort and a watch to display your power and record it into a workout file (the device that creates your workout file may also be known as a **Head Unit**, but I'll use the term Watch).

There are several alternatives for both of these items:

- Running Watch with wrist-based power. If you have an Apple Watch [Apple; Watch] or a recent running watch (e.g. [Garmin; Watch], [Coros; Watch], [Polar; Watch], [Suunto; Watch]), it may already include wrist-based power. The power meter is built into the watch. It may use GPS information, barometric pressure, information from local weather stations, and how your arms move when you run to model your power, recording the result in a workout file. Watches with wrist-based power are a budget-friendly choice, but if you include treadmill runs in your training, only Garmin offers wrist-based power for treadmill runs.

- Power-aware Running Watch. These don't have a built-in power meter – they need to be paired with a power meter (options below). They show your power numbers as you run and record those numbers and other metrics into a workout file that can be used for review and analysis. Most runners pair power meters with a watch (e.g., a Garmin or an Apple Watch), but it is possible to pair some power meters with a mobile phone.

- Footpod. Attaching to the laces on your shoe, power meter footpods (e.g. *[Stryd; Footpod]*) measure barometric pressure, temperature, wind speed and how your foot moves when you run to model your power, transmitting the result to your watch. Footpods can be paired to a watch (some can be paired to a mobile phone), and your watch may need an additional app to display your power numbers.

- Heart rate strap. These strap around your body and measure the way your body moves, transmitting the result to your watch, where the result is combined with GPS and barometric pressure to model your power. HR straps (e.g. *[Garmin; HRM]*) must be paired to a watch or other head unit to display your power number, and your watch will need an additional app to convert the sensor readings into power numbers.

- Running dynamics pods. Clipping to the rear waistband of your running shorts, the pod *[Garmin; Running Dynamics Pod]* is designed to measure your gait, but Garmin has added the ability to model your power. The pod must be paired to a Garmin watch, and you'll need a datafield *[Garmin; Running Power datafield]* to convert the sensor readings, combined with GPS and barometric pressure, into power numbers.

- Footbed power meter. A footbed power meter (e.g. *[RPM2; Footbed Power Meter]*) is designed to replace your running shoe insoles and measure your running form balance, but RPM2 has added the ability to model your power. The insoles must be paired to your mobile phone, and you'll need the Android or iOS app to convert the sensor readings into power numbers.

- Running Watch with a 3rd party datafield. Garmin watches enable 3rd party developers to add additional functionality to the watch – the RunPowerModel datafield *[Markus Holler; RunPowerModel datafield]* can be used by itself or in combination with a heart rate strap or running dynamics pod to obtain power numbers

Which power meter is "the best"?

At the time of writing, few studies have compared power meters, and the market is still developing, with new power meters being announced monthly.

☺ So far, based on a 2020 study [_Cerezuela-Espejo et al.; Are we ready to measure running power?_], the [_Stryd; Footpod_] is the power meter found to produce the most repeatable power numbers across a range of environments and conditions and the best validity compared to VO2 measurements.

Why do you need apps?

Running with Power is most effective when you're training for an event (I'll use the word "event" to include both competitive races and non-competitive events) using a training plan that includes higher-intensity workouts. Depending on your event, your plan may take ten weeks or more to prepare you appropriately. It may consist of a mix of easy and more challenging workouts, with perhaps three workouts per week at a minimum. That's three workouts per week (or more) over at least ten weeks – a minimum of thirty workouts.

The **Training** chapter covers how to plan your workouts.

So why mention them now?

Because that requires a lot of planning! Each workout may include sections at differing intensities and durations and weekly progressions that add intervals and adjust durations. This means you'll need to buy a plan with pre-built workouts, hire a coach who can provide pre-built workouts, or you'll want a planning app that enables you to build, schedule and save/reuse workouts quickly and easily.

That's also thirty or more completed workouts requiring consolidation into the metrics used to monitor your training. You'll want a reviewing app that makes this step quick and easy, and that provides meaningful power metrics so that you can focus on what your data means rather than on producing the metrics.

Finally, your planned workouts need to be transferred from your planning app to your watch before your run, and the completed workouts need to be transferred from your watch into your reviewing app after your run. Some apps entirely automate this transfer; others require a manual step or two.

★ In other words, your choices when getting started may significantly impact how much effort you'll have to put into planning and reviewing your training. Choices that work together will result in less effort; choices that don't work together or involve manual steps will result in more effort – when you'd rather be out running!

How to make the right choices

The next sections in this chapter present two different ways to choose your equipment and apps.

1. Choose a popular combination. If you don't want to spend time evaluating options, you can choose one of the popular combinations. The next two sections present combinations that have been proven to work for different running watches, along with the benefits and drawbacks of each.

2. Choose your own combination. If you don't want to use a ready-made solution, this chapter covers the five steps that take place for every workout and presents criteria for evaluating apps and equipment that support these steps. It also lists some better-known apps you may want to evaluate when choosing your combination. You can use the criteria and options as a starting point for your evaluation.

The Stryd Ecosystem

What's in this section?

NOTE: The following information was correct when this book was published but may now be outdated, given the speed with which Running with Power is evolving. If you have any questions about whether the following is accurate, please ask in the [f1r2a; Facebook Group].

The Stryd footpod is a power meter that can be used with any running watch. It provides power-based metrics, accurate speed and distance metrics and some additional metrics that can be used to assess how well you're converting effort into speed.

The Stryd Ecosystem is an end-to-end solution (from Planning through Reviewing) that works with running power. It provides the majority of the important power metrics and access to coaches and training plans.

It's a beginner-friendly way to start Running with Power.

What is it?

The [Stryd; Footpod] power meter attaches to your shoelaces. It measures how your foot moves when you run and must be paired to a watch or mobile phone to display your power number. It also produces several other metrics and can be paired both as a power meter and as a footpod to provide accurate speed and distance. It can be used outdoors and on a treadmill, using ANT+ or Bluetooth Low-Energy (BLE) connectivity.

Stryd (the company) has built a reasonably complete, power-focused ecosystem around the footpod, including:

- *[Stryd; PowerCenter]* – a web-based app to plan and review power-based workouts, available in free and subscription versions. With the subscription version, you can sign up for training plans (that come with pre-built workouts) or create your own workouts and use the full functionality of the PowerCenter to review your workouts and metrics. If you want to find a coach, it has a "find a coach" feature with listings from coaches using Stryd with their runners.

- *[Stryd; Mobile app]* – a mobile version of the PowerCenter.

- *[Stryd; Workout app]* – an Apple Watch app that can download and execute workouts.

- *[Stryd; Stryd Zones]* – a datafield for Garmin watches that lets you download and execute workouts while using other native Garmin features (like maps and navigation).

Benefits

- The entire ecosystem is designed from the ground up to work with running power.
- Works with full functionality on Garmin and Apple Watches and partial functionality on Coros, Polar, Wahoo and Suunto watches.

- The Stryd team have made it easy to get started using the *[Stryd; Footpod]*.

- The Stryd footpod is the power meter found to produce the most repeatable power numbers across a range of environments and conditions and to produce the best validity compared to VO2 measurements *[Cerezuela-Espejo et al.; Are we ready to measure running power?]*.

- Everything needed to produce metrics is on the footpod – there's no reliance on GPS or weather-station data.

- *[Stryd; PowerCenter]* provides most of the important power metrics.

- There is a large selection of power-based training plans included in the membership subscription, and the Stryd team frequently releases new workouts.

- There is a very active Facebook group *[Stryd; Facebook group]* and a responsive Stryd support team that handles issues and questions related to the ecosystem.

Drawbacks

- You'll need to buy a *[Stryd; Footpod]*, although there's a good second-hand market for the older versions.

- You'll need a membership to use all of the features of PowerCenter – the membership features are outlined on *[Stryd; Membership]* (click the "buy membership" button to see details).

- The ecosystem only supports power-based running workouts – if you are a multi-sport athlete, there's no support for cycling or swimming workouts. And if you sometimes run without your Stryd footpod, you won't be able to load those workouts into PowerCenter (although you can enter those workout details manually).

- [Stryd; PowerCenter] does not calculate Running Effectiveness (covered in the **Races & Events** chapter) or Reserve Work Capacity (covered in the **Power-Duration Curve** chapter). Its training load and intensity distribution metrics are presented differently than implementations in other parts f the power world – they're useful, just different (see the **Training** chapter for more on training metrics).

- The ecosystem was created for runners. Coaching functionality is slowly being added, but it's currently more limited than other coach-athlete platforms.

TrainingPeaks / WKO

What's in this section?

NOTE: The following information was correct when this book was published but may now be outdated, given the speed with which Running with Power is evolving. If you have any questions about whether the following is accurate, please ask in the [f1r2a; Facebook Group].

TrainingPeaks allows you to plan, track, and analyse your training all in one place. You can sync your account with your favourite apps and devices for real-time workout guidance and monitor your fitness progress with powerful data tools. Plus, training plans and coaching services guide you along the way.

WKO is an analysis tool that runs under MS Windows or on a Mac and provides a wide range of charts and graphs of your power data. You can also build your own using a powerful charting language. WKO integrates seamlessly with TrainingPeaks, syncing planned and completed workout data and a range of health metrics.

What is it?

TrainingPeaks (the company) has a fairly complete system for power-based (and non-power-based) training, including:

- [TrainingPeaks] – a website with hundreds of articles about training in general and training with power. If you want to find a coach, it has a "coach search" feature with listings from accredited coaches.

- [*TrainingPeaks; Training platform*] – a web-based app for planning training, building structured workouts, and reviewing workout and summary metrics. The app has an extensive list of integrations with other providers that support (in many cases) planned and completed workout transfers. The platform also supports coaches, who can see your calendar, create and schedule your workouts, and review your completed workouts.

- [*TrainingPeaks: Mobile App*] – a version of the Training Platform containing some of the features of the Training platform and additional features specific to the mobile app.

- [*WKO*] – an analysis tool that runs under MS Windows or on a Mac that provides a huge range of charts and graphs of your power data and the ability to build your own using a powerful charting language.

Benefits

- The system works with power and is fully multi-sport aware.

- Works with Garmin, Apple, Coros, Polar, Wahoo and Suunto watches.

- [*TrainingPeaks; Training platform*] and [*TrainingPeaks: Mobile App*] display all the important power metrics. In fact, the team behind TrainingPeaks originated many of the power-based metrics in use today.

- There are integrations with many watch manufacturers that make downloading and uploading workouts straightforward.
- There's a large selection of power-based training plans (available for an additional fee).
- There's a large database of accredited running coaches – if you're looking for a coach who understands how to Run with Power, you'll find one here. The coach can use a coaching account on TrainingPeaks to plan and deliver your training workouts.

Drawbacks

- You'll need a premium subscription to use all of the features of the Training Platform – the premium features are outlined on [*TrainingPeaks; Premium*]. It is possible to use the free version for most things apart from building custom workouts.
- You'll need to buy a separate license for WKO if you want to take advantage of the advanced analytics and custom chart builder.
- WKO has a steep learning curve if you want to take full advantage of the custom chart functionality (although you can, of course, use charts that others have already built).

Choose your own combination

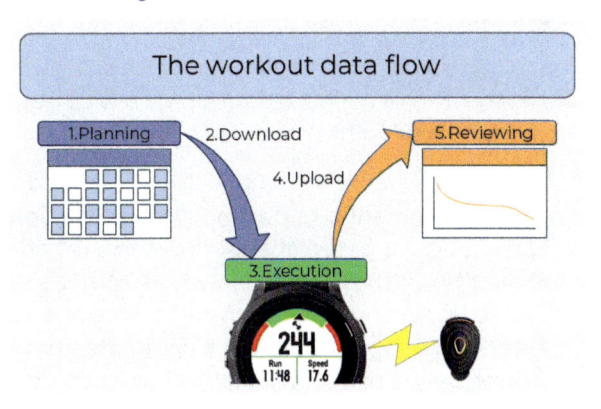

The workout data flow

What's in this section?

There are five steps (shown in the diagram above) that take place for every workout: Planning, Download, Execution, Upload and Reviewing

☺ This section presents criteria that can be used to evaluate apps that automate these steps. The criteria can be used as-is or as a starting point for your own evaluation criteria.

This section also lists some of the better-known apps you may want to evaluate when choosing your combination.

Criteria for evaluating equipment and app choices

The diagram at the beginning of this section shows the flow of workout data for each workout – it has the following five steps:

1. Planning – Some workouts (like a long run) don't need planning, but many have multiple steps, each targeted at specific intensities and durations – these are known as structured workouts. Workout planning can be done by someone else (using pre-built workouts from a power-based plan or a coach), or you can do it yourself using your choice of Planning app.

2. Download – Transferring a planned workout from your planning app to your watch.

3. Execution – To maximise a workout's benefit, you'll need to run to the target intensities (or intensity ranges) and durations. Ideally, your watch or power meter comes with an app that will guide you through structured workouts. You may also choose to use another app instead of the app provided by your equipment vendor.

4. Upload – Transferring a completed workout from your watch to your Reviewing app.

5. Reviewing – Your reviewing app should enable you to examine the tree (your individual workouts) and examine the forest (providing key metrics based on consolidated data from completed and planned workouts). It should

also enable you to check that your training is on track and to identify adjustments you might need to make if it's not.

Examining each of these areas in detail, here are some criteria you might use to evaluate each option, starting with the most important step, Execution, as your on-watch experience is crucial.

Execution

Your on-watch experience is crucial. With the proper setup, you'll be guided through a structured workout with clear targets (using colours, alerts or audible prompts) and durations. If it's not right, you may wonder what targets you should be running to or what workout step is next.

Here are some criteria you can use to assess whether to use the app that came with your equipment or whether to look for an alternative:

- Do you want to see two (or more) power-based metrics on one display (e.g. 3-second power alongside lap power)?

- Do you want to see non-power metrics (e.g. HR, pace, distance) on the same display as power-based metrics?

- Do you want a visual display showing when you're on target (vs. above or below target) – perhaps a "power gauge" layout?

- Do you have any restrictions to your vision that might mean you need contrasting colours or large fonts?

- Do you want audible or vibration alerts when you're above/below your target range or your workout is moving to the next step?

- Do you want to use other watch features (e.g. maps, music) while executing a structured workout?

- How much does it cost to use the app or datafield?

Planning & Download

When planning workouts, there are three areas to consider: the ease of use of the planning app, the workouts that the app produces, and how to download planned workouts onto your watch. Here are the criteria you can use for each of these areas.

For the ease of use of the app:

- Do you want to build workouts on your mobile phone or using a web-based interface?

- Do you need to be able to move workouts between days to adjust for "life happening"?

- Do you want to set up re-usable workouts that you can drag/drop onto a calendar?

- How much does it cost to use the structured workout planning functionality?

- Do you want to buy/use a training plan that is only available on a specific platform?

For the structured workouts it produces:

- Do you want to set targets using watts, percentage of CP/FTP or both?
- Do you want to set specific targets, target ranges, or both?
- Do you want to plan by duration, distance, or both?
- Do you want some workout sections to continue until you press the lap button?
- Do you want to be able to plan repeating steps (2-step, 3-step, 4-step) or progressing steps?

For the workout download onto your watch:

- Is there a way to download a workout created using your planning app onto your watch (there may not be)?
- Is the download "automatic" – once connected, workouts magically appear on your watch just before you need them?
- If not automatic, is there an easy manual download that doesn't involve transferring files?
- If you have to transfer files, how easy is it, and how long does it take?

Upload & Reviewing

When reviewing workout data, there are three areas to consider: the ease of use of the reviewing app, the metrics and analysis that the app produces, and how to upload completed workouts. Here are the criteria you can use for each of these areas.

For the ease of use of the reviewing app:

- Does it present different views of your data appropriate to the review you want to do – for example, a calendar of completed workouts, individual workout data, or metrics calculated from multiple workouts?

- Does it enable you to zoom in on specific workout sections to see metrics for the individual sections?

- Does it present workout summary metrics and the supporting details from which they were calculated?

- How much does it cost?

For the metrics and analysis:

- Does it enable you to see whether individual workouts were executed as planned?

- Does it show a variety of workout metrics apart from power (e.g. Running Effectiveness, Reserve Work Capacity)?

- Does it calculate your Critical Power or Functional Threshold Power – a fundamental metric used by almost all the other power-based metrics?

- Does it calculate training load metrics – so that you can monitor your training load balance?

- Does it calculate training intensities – so that you can monitor your training intensity distribution?

For the workout upload into the app:

- Is there a way to upload completed workouts from your watch into the app (often, this is via another app)?

- Is the upload "automatic" – once connected, completed workout data magically appears in the app?

- If not automatic, is there an easy manual upload that doesn't involve transferring files?

- If you have to transfer files, how easy is it, and how long does it take?

- If you lose or forget to record a workout, can you include the workout in training load metrics by manually adding workout details (including distance, duration and an estimate of average power)?

Some options you may want to explore

NOTE: The following information was correct when this book was published but may now be outdated, given the speed with which Running with Power is evolving. If you have any questions about whether the following is accurate, please ask in the [f1r2a; Facebook Group].

The following is a list of some of the better-known apps that you may want to evaluate when choosing your own combination:

Multi-step

- *[Today's Plan]* – is subscription-based, offers a training plan library (or you can build your own workouts and training plan), syncs planned workouts to some platforms and completed workouts from many other platforms, offers a mobile app with activity recording (if you don't have a watch), and includes an extensive range of analytics. If you're a coach, it also includes integrated coach-athlete functionality.

- [Watchletic] – there are free and paid versions. The free version lets you plan structured workouts, create workout plans (in Watchletic), execute them on your Apple Watch, and then sync completed workouts to TrainingPeaks, Final Surge and others. The paid version supports importing workouts planned in TrainingPeaks, Final Surge and others.

- [iSmoothRun] – is subscription-based and supports workout and training schedule planning (also importing from TrainingPeaks and Final Surge) and on-watch execution for the Apple Watch. Completed workouts can be synced to many popular running sites.

- [intervals.icu] – free of charge, it analyses your rides, runs, swims and other activities (with and without power). It provides basic and advanced analytics and planning in an easy-to-use web interface with support for desktops, phones and tablets.

- [Sport Tracks] – this subscription-based multi-sport app has a training calendar to plan upcoming workouts and analyses completed workouts to provide per-workout and multi-workout metrics.

Planning & Download

- [*Final Surge*] (beta version) – free for athletes, the website offers the ability to plan power-based workouts, to use pre-built workouts and training plans (some free, some paid), to download power-based workouts to Apple Watch and other running watches, and to see individual workout metrics (but not metrics calculated over multiple workouts). If you're a coach, it also includes integrated coach-athlete functionality.

Execution

- [*Garmin; RunPowerWorkout datafield*] – free of charge, this Garmin datafield allows you to follow structured workouts based on Power on Garmin watches that support Connect IQ 3.2. It can show power and non-power metrics using different layouts and can be set up to trigger alerts if you run outside of the target range.

- [*Garmin; RunPowerModel datafield*] – free of charge, this Garmin datafield provides wrist-based power on watches that don't have that capability. Designed with trail runners in mind, it can be used for road or trail running and has several parameters (e.g. backpack weight) that can be adjusted per run.

Upload & Reviewing

- *[Golden Cheetah]* – free of charge (open source), this PC/Mac/Linux app imports workout files from many sources (some automated, some manual) and provides a rich set of analysis tools, including Critical Power modelling (and your Power-Duration curve), calculation of Reserve Work Capacity (called W' in Golden Cheetah) as well as training load and intensity distribution.

- *[Elevate]* – free of charge, this Chrome extension integrates with your Strava data to provide workout-specific and multi-workout trends and data.

Making the connections

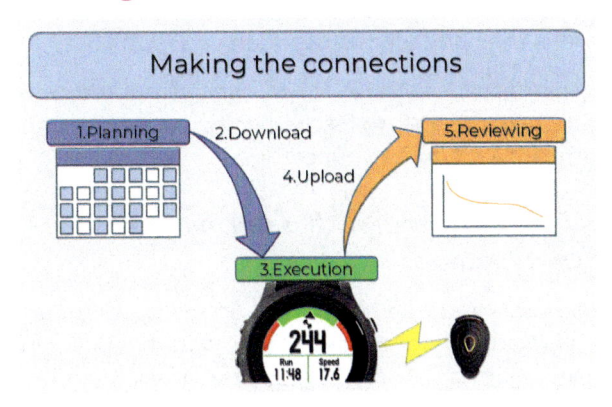

What's in this section?

You'll need to connect your apps if you want planned workouts to download to your watch and completed workouts to upload from your watch.

The tables below outline the process for some typical setups, or can be used to think through the setup for your combination of apps.

Reducing your manual effort

Whatever equipment and apps you choose, you'll most likely need to make some connections between them so that planned and completed workouts flow automatically, with minimal need for manual steps.

A few examples are presented in the tables below, along with links to help pages describing how to make the connections between your apps.

If your setup isn't one of the ones presented, you can use the examples below to work through similar thinking for your setup.

Stryd ecosystem with a Garmin and a Stryd footpod

The preferred app for using a Stryd power meter on a Garmin is the Stryd Zones data field, which uses Garmin Connect to download planned workouts to your watch and upload completed workouts from your watch.

Coupled with the Stryd ecosystem for planning and reviewing, this gives the following setup:

Step	App
1.Planning	Stryd ecosystem
2.Download	Stryd ecosystem to Garmin Connect
3.Execution	Stryd Zones datafield (in a "run" profile)
4.Upload	Garmin Connect to Stryd ecosystem
5.Reviewing	Stryd ecosystem

To connect your Stryd account to your Garmin account, see *[Stryd; Stryd Zones Data Fields and Garmin Watch Setup]*

Stryd ecosystem with an Apple Watch and a Stryd footpod

The preferred app for using a Stryd power meter on an Apple Watch is the *[Stryd; Workout app]*, which communicates directly with the Stryd ecosystem to download the next five days of planned workouts to your watch and upload completed workouts.

Coupled with the Stryd ecosystem for planning and reviewing, this gives the following setup:

Step	App
1.Planning	Stryd ecosystem
2.Download	Stryd ecosystem to Stryd Workout app
3.Execution	Stryd Workout app
4.Upload	Stryd Workout app to Stryd ecosystem
5.Reviewing	Stryd ecosystem

TrainingPeaks with a Garmin and a Stryd footpod

The preferred app for using a Stryd power meter on a Garmin is the *[Stryd; Stryd Zones]* datafield, which uses Garmin Connect to download planned workouts to your watch and upload completed workouts.

Coupled with TrainingPeaks for planning and reviewing, this gives the following setup:

Step	App
1.Planning	TrainingPeaks (web app)
2.Download	TrainingPeaks to Garmin Connect
3.Execution	Stryd Zones datafield (in a "run" profile)
4.Upload	Garmin Connect to TrainingPeaks
5.Reviewing	TrainingPeaks

To connect your TrainingPeaks account to your Garmin account, see *[TrainingPeaks; Sync Your Garmin and TrainingPeaks Accounts]*.

TrainingPeaks with an Apple Watch and a Stryd footpod

The preferred app for using a Stryd power meter on an Apple Watch is the *[Stryd; Workout app]*, which communicates directly with the Stryd ecosystem to download the next five days of planned workouts to your watch and upload completed workouts.

Coupled with TrainingPeaks for planning and reviewing, this gives the following setup:

Step	App
1.Planning	TrainingPeaks (web app)
2a.Download	TrainingPeaks to Stryd ecosystem
2b.Download	Stryd ecosystem to Stryd Workout app
3.Execution	Stryd Workout app
4a.Upload	Stryd Workout app to Stryd ecosystem
4a.Upload	Stryd ecosystem to TrainingPeaks
5.Reviewing	TrainingPeaks

To connect your Stryd account to your TrainingPeaks account, see *[Stryd; Connecting to TrainingPeaks]*. You should choose to "Export Activities to" and "Import Workouts from". Note that the connection syncs information twice daily – if you want to trigger an immediate sync, you should choose "Manually Sync Workouts".

Using WKO for advanced analytics

For advanced analytics, WKO can be added to either of the TrainingPeaks setups shown above, giving the following steps:

Step	App
1.Planning	TrainingPeaks (web app)
2.Download	See above
3.Execution	See above
4ab.Upload	... to TrainingPeaks
4c.Upload	TrainingPeaks to WKO
5.Reviewing	WKO

To connect WKO to your TrainingPeaks account, see [[WKO; Managing Athletes](#)] (then choose the download tab).

Is it complicated to start Running with Power?

What's in this section?

You may be thinking that is complicated to start Running with Power or that power meters or power-capable watches are expensive.

But it doesn't have to be the case.

☺ It is possible to start with a simple setup, then adjust your setup when you need to – or if you don't, stay with the setup that suits your needs. The options might be:

Keep it simple – Stryd

Buy a Stryd power meter. Use the Stryd app on a mobile or Apple watch – whatever equipment you already have.

Sync all workouts to Stryd PowerCenter (PC) and use Auto-CP, Stryd training zones, and PowerCenter for workout analysis.

Follow a Stryd training plan.

For race targets, use Stryd's Race Power Calculator (found in the IOS/Android Stryd apps) or Stryd's Race Calculator (found in PowerCenter) *[Stryd; Race Calculator]*.

Keep it simple – Wrist-based power

Buy a running watch with wrist-based power.

Buy a power-based training plan *[Final Surge: Training Plans]* or use Final Surge *[Final Surge: Beta platform]* to plan your workouts. Connect Final Surge to your running watch provider's platform.

Ensure your training includes a variety of maximal efforts at different durations.

Use a free reviewing app (e.g. *[Golden Cheetah]*, *[intervals.icu]*) to review your workouts and obtain key power metrics, connecting the reviewing app to your running watch provider's platform.

Use SuperPower Calculator's "Race Power Scenario Planning" for race targets *[SPC for Sheets]* or *[SPC for Web]*.

Get into the data

Include CP testing in your training (covered in the **Fundamentals** chapter).

Investigate/use additional systems (e.g. TrainingPeaks, WKO) for post-workout analysis, including the use of additional power metrics: Running Effectiveness, Reserve Work Capacity (RWC), Form Power, Riegel Exponent, etc. Additional power metrics are covered in the **Training** and **Races & Events** chapters.

Use SuperPower Calculator's "Race Power Scenario Planning" for race targets *[SPC for Sheets]* or *[SPC for Web]*, using RE and RWC for shorter events, or RE and your Riegel Exponent for longer events.

Understand your underlying physiology

Research the link between power and your underlying physiology – what happens as you run and how that's reflected in the numbers and in the training prescriptions.

While this might seem more suitable for running coaches, athletes can also benefit from this.

☺ The Empirical Cycling podcast *[[Empirical Cycling; Podcast](#)]* is a great place to start. While the information is based on cycling, there are many good insights about the physiology behind training with power that translate to running.

Chapter 3

Fundamentals

What's coming up?

There is a reason this chapter is called Fundamentals.

It presents the foundation for many other Running with Power metrics.

Once you understand the concepts in this chapter, the rest of Running with Power should fall nicely into place.

Here's a summary of what the chapter covers ...

We start with a little physiology – how your body responds to exercise at different intensities, including the Threshold below which you can sustain the intensity for more than 30 minutes or so and above which you can't sustain the intensity and have to slow down or stop (typically in 30 minutes or less).

Training (or detraining) can move your Threshold, and it's essential to track your Threshold movements so that you can adjust your training and racing targets. Identifying your Threshold used to require lab-based testing; with power, its location can be determined using field-based tests to obtain your CP/FTP, a measure of your metabolic fitness found at or about your Threshold.

There are many different protocols and models for estimating CP/FTP. Some are more valid (aligned to physiology) and, therefore, more useful than others. This chapter presents the three most valid/useful: Critical Power (CP), Functional Threshold Power (FTP), and Auto-Critical Power (Auto-CP). This chapter explains the differences between the three and how to calculate each.

All three tests are based on similar concepts and aim to identify the Threshold power level (to within a few percentage points). Given their similarity, this book uses the term CP/FTP to refer to the three field-based tests in general and to the power level that they identify.

The chapter also covers which CP/FTP to use and, if you use more than one, how to compare and cross-check each result against the others before deciding which CP/FTP value to use.

It concludes with the importance of maintaining your CP/FTP by including regular CP tests or maximum effort runs in your training (depending on your CP/FTP choice).

What happens when you exercise?

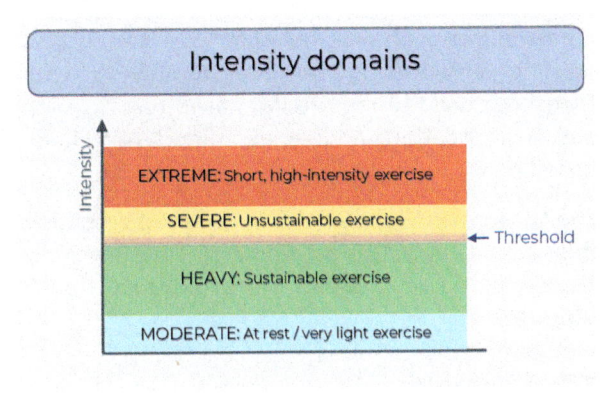

Intensity domains

- **EXTREME:** Short, high-intensity exercise
- **SEVERE:** Unsustainable exercise ← Threshold
- **HEAVY:** Sustainable exercise
- **MODERATE:** At rest / very light exercise

What's in this section?

★ Research into how your body responds to exercise at different intensities has identified that exercise below a certain intensity can be sustained for relatively long periods (more than 30 minutes or so up to hours or days). In comparison, exercise above a certain intensity quickly leads to a need to slow down or stop (typically within 30 minutes or so).

★ The change from being able to sustain the exercise to having to slow down or stop doesn't happen at a precise point. Instead, it's a phase transition, with many metabolic changes occurring at different rates and in parallel over a small range of intensities. I'll use the term **Threshold** as shorthand for this phase transition.

★ With training (or detraining), your Threshold can move. When training, it's essential to track your Threshold movements so that you can adjust training and racing targets. Identifying your Threshold used to require lab-based testing; with power, its location can be determined using field-based tests.

The three most valid/useful field-based tests and their results are: Critical Power (CP), Functional Threshold Power (FTP), and Auto-Critical Power (Auto-CP).

Effort domains

Power is a measure of *how hard* you're running (your **intensity**), which results from the energy/effort you put into your run.

Knowing how your body copes with different intensities is essential for fully understanding power-based concepts. The following briefly summarises *[Burnley; Exercise intensity domains and phase transitions]*.

If you run at lower intensity levels, you can sustain the intensity for an extended period, typically more than 30 minutes, and your body achieves a metabolic steady(ish) state. Steady(ish) means that there are variations in your metabolism, but they work to maintain the intensity at which you're running. Researchers call these domains "moderate to heavy."

Researchers use blood lactate to differentiate between moderate and heavy, but an easy way to tell the difference when running is to use the "talk test" – if you can hold a conversation while running, you're running at a moderate intensity; if not, you're running at a heavy intensity.

If, instead, you run at higher intensity levels, you won't be able to achieve a metabolic steady(ish) state. You'll begin to fatigue much more rapidly and need to slow down or stop – typically within 30 minutes. Researchers call the domains where you fatigue much more quickly "severe to extreme domains."

The change from heavy to severe doesn't happen at a precise point – it's a **phase transition** within a narrow range of intensities, with lots of metabolic changes occurring at different rates and in parallel (I'll use the term **Threshold** as shorthand for this phase transition). Researchers have identified several markers that can be lab-tested to identify this Threshold – one well-known marker is Maximum Lactate Steady State (**MLSS**), which is "the maximum constant concentration of lactase reached during sustained high-activity" [Wikipedia; Steady State (Biochemistry)], but there are many others.

VO2max, which is "the maximum rate of oxygen consumption attainable during physical exertion" [_Wikipedia; VO2 max_], is above Threshold, but it too does not have a single point at which it occurs, and it cannot be reached from all intensities above Threshold (some intensities are too high and lead to fatigue failure before VO2max is attained). There is broad acceptance among researchers that intensities above VO2max are extreme, while intensities below VO2max are severe, but this differentiation is not universally used.

★ Threshold is an important intensity range, as intensities above that range _will_ lead to fatigue failure if the duration is too long. This is why training at higher intensities is usually achieved using intervals with recovery periods.

Your Threshold can also move with training or lack of training (detraining) – it's a measure of your metabolic fitness. This means it's essential to track Threshold movements when training.

This chapter describes how you can identify your Threshold using field-based tests that you can complete yourself rather than lab-based tests.

I use **CP/FTP** to refer to the Threshold that any (and all) the field-based tests aim to identify.

Why is it essential to be able to identify and track CP/FTP?

★ CP/FTP is a fundamental power metric. It's a measure of your metabolic fitness, and it's used:

- to target training intensities aimed at stimulating adaptations specific to your goal race
- when monitoring training load to reduce the risk of injury and to plan an ideal taper
- when taking part in an event, to set a target that reflects your event-day fitness and that takes into account the event environment, adjusting for heat, humidity and altitude if necessary

Critical Power (CP)

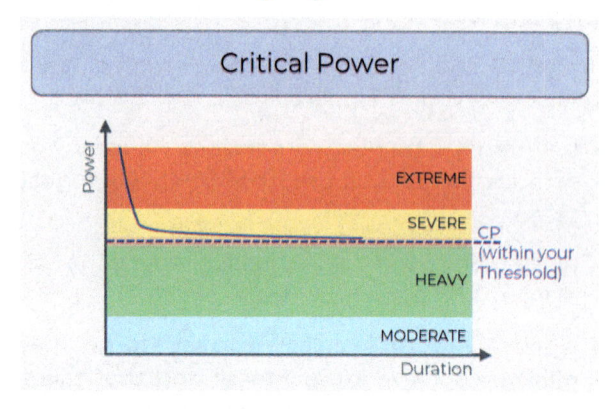

Critical Power chart showing Power vs Duration with zones: EXTREME, SEVERE, HEAVY, MODERATE, and CP line (within your Threshold).

What's in this section?

Critical Power was initially identified through research on muscle fibres. The concept was later extended and validated for whole-body exercise.

You can identify your Critical Power using a CP test. The CP test also identifies your Reserve Work Capacity (RWC), which measures how long you can maintain work above CP.

★ CP is a measure of your metabolic fitness. When training, you can track changes in your CP by regularly re-testing.

What is it?

Critical Power (**CP**) is defined in *[Monod and Scherrer; The Work Capacity of a Synergic Muscular Group]* as "an exercise intensity that could be sustained for a very long time".

Originally based on research into single muscle groups, further research extended and validated the CP concept for whole-body exercise *[Hill; The Critical Power Concept]* while noting that "for a very long time" was usually 30 to 60 minutes of exercise at CP.

Why is it needed?

So that you can use field-based CP testing to identify your Threshold.

The research identified a hyperbolic relationship between power output and the time it can be sustained – the solid blue line (with a bend in it) in the chart at the beginning of this section.

The power level that the horizontal end of the solid blue line approaches (but never meets) is your Critical Power (CP). This power level is within the phase transition and is shown as a dotted blue line in the chart at the beginning of this section.

How to measure or calculate it?

CP can be calculated using a CP test.

A CP test is usually a single workout that includes two maximum effort sections – one short (typically 3 minutes) and one long (typically 10 minutes or more).

Why these durations? *[Maturana et al.; Critical power: How different protocols and models affect its determination]* found that "CP was considerably overestimated when only trials lasting less than 10 minutes were included", and *[Palladino; Understanding and Applying CP Testing for Runners]* recommends "a 3-minute and 10-minute test protocol – at a minimum" and "for stronger, more experienced runners, and those that have sufficient fatigue resistance ... a testing protocol with durations of 3 minutes, and 12, 15, or 20 minutes".

[Palladino; Protocol for CP testing] also recommends executing the short-duration effort before executing the long-duration effort to avoid underperforming the short-duration effort, which would result in an overestimated CP.

Once the test is complete, you can calculate CP using the following formula:

CP = ((long test AP * long test S) – (short test AP * short test S)) / (long test S – short test S)

where AP is the Average Power, and S is the duration in seconds.

You can also use SuperPower Calculator for Sheets [SPC for Sheets] or SuperPower Calculator for the Web [SPC for Web] to calculate your CP using your test results.

Note: The result of the CP calculation will always be a lower power than either of the pairs used to calculate it. this means CP must be calculated using higher-intensity power-duration pairs. It's not correct (and not useful) to try to calculate CP using results from events (or power-duration pairs) lasting longer than 30 minutes, e.g., a half-marathon, 10k, or a slower 5k.

How to use it?

You use your Critical Power to:

- set workout targets – relative to CP, targeting adaptations aligned to your goal event
- monitor your training load – relative to CP to reduce injury risk
- set race/event targets – based on completed workouts
- estimate finish times – using additional workout metrics

Functional Threshold Power (FTP)

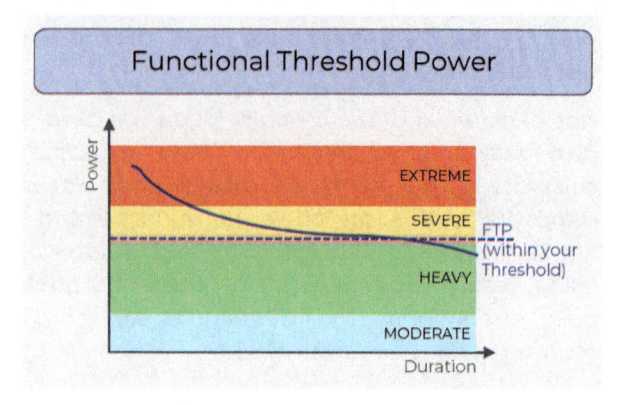

Functional Threshold Power

Power vs Duration chart showing zones: EXTREME, SEVERE, HEAVY, MODERATE, with FTP (within your Threshold) marked at the boundary between SEVERE and HEAVY.

What's in this section?

Functional Threshold Power was developed in the cycling world to solve several problems related to the notion of "threshold" in sports performance.

FTP is calculated using a multi-parameter mathematical model.

★ FTP is a measure of your metabolic fitness. When training, you can track changes in your FTP by regularly running max efforts at various durations and feeding the completed workouts into *[TrainingPeaks]* or *[WKO]*.

What is it?

Functional Threshold Power (**FTP**) is "the highest power that an athlete can maintain in a quasi-steady state without fatiguing" *[Allen, Coggan & McGregor; Functional Threshold Power]*.

Steve Palladino, in *[Palladino; Running FTP - A Primer]*, applies this to running: "the highest power that a runner can maintain in a quasi-steady state without fatiguing, where the duration may range from 30-70 minutes, depending on the individual".

Why is it needed?

So that you can use completed workout data, including maximum effort runs at various intensities, to identify your Threshold.

Initially developed by Andrew Coggan, PhD, and first presented to USA cycling coaches in 2003, Functional Threshold Power:

- removes the need for lab testing to determine threshold
- standardises the definition of threshold
- establishes threshold as a practical, functional way to assess performance

[Allen, Coggan & McGregor; Functional Threshold Power] fully describes FTP and includes additional methods for estimating it. It notes that Critical Power (CP) "is often very close to FTP in terms of power".

Viewed graphically (see the chart at the beginning of this section), FTP is the dotted blue line crossing the solid blue curve at the point where it drops after flattening horizontally. The solid blue curve is your Power-Duration Curve, which is covered in the **Power-Duration Curve** chapter.

FTP is within the phase transition from Heavy to Severe, which means that FTP can be used to identify the location of your Threshold.

How to measure or calculate it?

FTP is calculated using a multi-parameter mathematical model.

The FTP calculation uses completed workout data, identifying power maximums for various durations across multiple workouts to feed into the model.

☺ The calculation typically uses data from the last 90 days of training, and to ensure a valid FTP, your maximum efforts should cover a range of durations – for example, 10-20 seconds, 2-3 minutes, 10-12 minutes; 20-30 minutes or a 5k race. To ensure that no maximum efforts drop out of the 90-day window, you should run maximum efforts every 4 -5 weeks (alternating across the durations).

How to use it?

You use your Functional Threshold Power to:

- set workout targets – relative to FTP, targeting adaptations aligned to your goal event
- monitor your training load – relative to FTP to reduce injury risk
- set race/event targets – based on completed workouts
- estimate finish times – using additional workout metrics

Auto-Calculated Critical Power (Auto-CP)

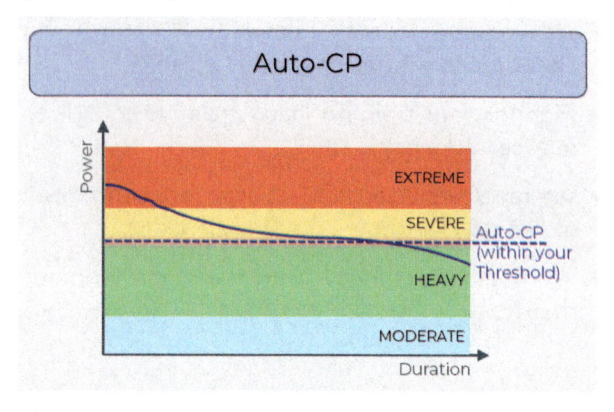

What's in this section?

Auto-Calculated Critical Power is a Stryd innovation *[Stryd; Auto-CP]* that calculates your Critical Power using completed workout data uploaded to the Stryd ecosystem.

Auto-CP is calculated using a multi-parameter mathematical model *[Stryd; PowerCenter]*.

★ Auto-CP is a measure of your metabolic fitness. When training, you can track changes in your Auto-CP by regularly running max efforts at various durations and feeding the completed workouts into PowerCenter *[Stryd; PowerCenter]*.

What is it?

Auto-Calculated Critical Power (**Auto-CP**) is a Stryd innovation *[Stryd; Auto-CP]* that calculates your Critical Power using completed workout data uploaded to the Stryd ecosystem so that your Critical Power is automatically calculated from your recent training data.

Why is it needed?

So that you can use completed workout data, including maximum effort runs at various intensities, to identify your Threshold.

Auto-CP means that:

- Stryd power zones are always accurate and up-to-date
- you have a realistic understanding of your current fitness heading into race day
- Critical Power testing (running multiple max efforts in a single workout or a single week) is not necessary as long as your training includes maximal runs at a range of durations
- you will have a better idea of your running training load due to more accurate Running Stress Scores

Viewed graphically (see the chart at the beginning of this section), Auto-CP is the dotted blue line crossing the solid blue curve at the point where it drops after flattening horizontally – the solid blue curve is your Power-Duration Curve and is covered in the **Power-Duration Curve** chapter.

Auto-CP is within the phase transition from Heavy to Severe, which means that Auto-CP can be used to identify the location of your Threshold.

The Stryd Power-Duration Curve (found on the [Stryd; PowerCenter]) also shows which workouts were used to model the curve, colour-coding them so that you can identify any areas based on older workouts where you may need to schedule a fresh maximum effort in your training.

How to measure or calculate it?

Auto-CP is calculated using a multi-parameter mathematical model [Stryd; PowerCenter].

The Auto-CP calculation uses completed workout data, identifying power maximums for several durations across multiple workouts to feed into the model.

☺ The calculation typically uses data from the last 90 days of training, and to ensure a valid Auto-CP, your maximum efforts should cover a range of durations – for example, 10-20 seconds, 2-3 minutes, 10-12 minutes; 20-30 minutes or a 5k race. To ensure that no maximum efforts drop out of the 90-day window, you should run maximum efforts every 4-5 weeks (alternating across the durations).

[Palladino; How does Stryd Auto-CP work?] contains more detail on Auto-CP.

How to use it?

You use your Auto-calculated Critical Power to:

- set workout targets – relative to Auto-CP, targeting adaptations aligned to your goal event

- monitor your training load – relative to Auto-CP to reduce injury risk

- set race/event targets – based on completed workouts

- estimate finish times – using additional workout metrics

Which CP/FTP should you use?

What's in this section?

All three estimation/calculation methods are based on similar concepts, aiming to identify your Threshold (to within a few percentage points). I use the term **CP/FTP** to refer to the Threshold that these field-based tests identify.

CP/FTP represents your metabolic fitness – how well-adapted your metabolism is to running. It may increase as you train or decrease as you detrain. It's a useful indicator of your training progress (but it's not the only indicator).

If you use more than one test, each may give a slightly different result due to differences in the testing protocol, how the results are modelled, or how testing was executed. You can use the variation to compare and cross-check the individual results against the others before deciding which CP/FTP value to use.

To ensure your testing results in a usable CP/FTP, you shouldn't combine results from different power meters or adjust any height or weight settings in your power meter configuration. If you do, you'll end up with a CP/FTP using numbers calculated from different bases.

Keep in mind that CP/FTP represents an *approximation* of the Threshold's position (to within a few percentage points). Its usefulness isn't due to its precision; it's that it enables runners to use field-based testing to identify their Threshold and monitor their metabolic fitness.

CP, FTP and Auto-CP are similar

★ If you've read the previous three sections, you've probably realised that CP, FTP and Auto-CP are very similar.

They:

- base their calculations on maximal effort runs at two or more higher-intensity durations

- identify a power level that's within the phase transition between the heavy and severe domains

- produce a number that can be used for setting training targets, monitoring training load, setting race/event targets and estimating race/event finish times

☺ The CP/FTP you choose to use will most likely depend on your choice of equipment and apps:

- If you use a *[Stryd; Footpod]* and the Stryd Ecosystem, you'll probably use Auto-CP.

- If you purchased *[WKO]* or are training with a coach that uses TrainingPeaks, you'll probably use FTP.

- If you have neither (or if you run CP tests), you'll probably use CP testing and SuperPower Calculator for Sheets *[SPC for Sheets]* or SuperPower Calculator for the Web *[SPC for Web]* to calculate CP.

What are the differences?

If you use more than one test, each may give slightly different results. The differences come from:

- Protocol – the max efforts from which the calculation is made, including whether the max efforts are run individually or two or more during the same workout, the recovery between the max efforts (within the same workout or across several days or weeks), and if running a CP test, the order in which you ran the tests.

- Model – the calculation itself, including how many max efforts are included and whether the model uses a line of best fit (CP, FTP) or a line across the maximums (Auto-CP).

- Execution – how you ran the max efforts, including how well you followed the protocol, whether you were fresh/fatigued when you ran them, whether the efforts were outside or on a treadmill, and whether the environmental conditions were similar.

In addition, if you change your power meter or the settings used to calibrate the power meter, you may end up with an unusable CP/FTP. This is because:

- Power Meter differences – there is no standard way to calculate running power. There are differences due to the placement of the power meter (foot, wrist, or torso), whether the calculation includes or excludes elastic recoil, how the calculation handles weight and height, the sensor sample rate, and so on. In short, power readings from different power meters (even different generations of the same power meter) will give different results and should not be combined.

- Weight and Height setting – depending on how the power meter calculates a power reading, combining results that use different weight or height settings may lead to a CP/FTP using numbers calculated from differing bases.

Which number is correct?

CP/FTP is not a precise measurement.

It represents a phase transition, indicating the power at or around which your body will experience several metabolic changes and above which you will begin to fatigue much more quickly.

★ Which means that you should not expect there to be a single correct number.

Instead, if your testing gives you two or more numbers, use the variation to compare and cross-check the individual results against the others before deciding which CP/FTP value to use.

☺ Note that using a slightly lower value in your training reduces your injury risk and can build momentum and confidence in your workout outcomes.

Is CP/FTP meaningful?

Do the differences in the numbers and the methods used to calculate them mean that it's impossible to calculate a meaningful CP/FTP?

No.

CP/FTP numbers represent an *approximation* (within a few percentage points) of your Threshold. The approximation is due to how our bodies work – it's a phase transition, not a clean cutover.

Even though it's an approximation, it's possible (with careful planning and a good choice of data and calculation method) to obtain numbers that are consistent with previous training blocks, meaningful for the next training block, and give insights into your training progression.

★ The usefulness of CP/FTP is that it aligns with your underlying physiology, it can be determined without the need for laboratory equipment or blood testing, and that your individual CP/FTP can be monitored as it changes (due to training or detraining) by including CP tests or max effort runs in your training schedule.

★ CP/FTP is a practical, field-based, individualised way to identify *your* Threshold.

Maintaining a valid CP/FTP

What's in this section?

Your Threshold moves with training (or detraining). You should ensure that you maintain your CP/FTP by including regular CP tests or maximum effort runs in your training (depending on your CP/FTP choice).

If you haven't trained recently, you can estimate CP/FTP using the average power from 3 easy runs and an assumption that the intensity of those runs is approximately 80% of CP/FTP.

If you are a multi-sport athlete, you should calculate CP/FTP separately for each sport. You should also maintain training load metrics per sport rather than combining numbers across different sports.

CP/FTP relies on maximum-effort runs

CP/FTP is calculated using maximum efforts. As the name suggests, your maximum efforts are the highest effort you can maintain for a specific duration. For example, your 3-minute maximum effort is the maximum power you maintained for 3 minutes (elapsed) from all runs in the last 90 days. If you manage a higher 3-minute maximum effort tomorrow, that new maximum effort will replace your previous 3-minute maximum in the CP/FTP calculation.

The number of different durations included in the CP/FTP calculation depends on the CP/FTP choice

– a CP test has two maximum efforts, while modelled FTP and Auto-CP monitor all your completed workouts to identify maximum efforts across a range of durations over the last 90 days.

★ This means that your training schedule should include CP tests or maximum effort runs, ideally at the start of a training cycle, every 4-6 weeks within a training cycle, and around two weeks before you run your goal event.

☺ It's also important to note that when using the FTP or Auto-CP calculations, the maximum efforts should be executed under similar conditions to avoid variances from heat, humidity, altitude, wind, outdoor vs. treadmill, etc. Ideally, they should also be performed over a flat route to prevent issues from hills.

Will CP tests or maximum efforts mean I'll miss a training run?

No.

Maximum effort runs are runs at higher intensities, which should be part of any training plan.

In the words of Andrew Coggan, PhD, "testing is training too".

Why has my CP/FTP decreased?

The most obvious reason your CP/FTP has decreased is that you're detraining. This means you won't be as metabolically fit as you were, and your CP tests or maximum effort runs will reflect this in a lower CP/FTP.

Another reason your CP/FTP has decreased is if you've included a new maximum effort at a shorter duration (typically durations less than 3-5 minutes). In this case, the calculation will reflect the improvement as an increase in your ability to run short durations and a decrease in your ability to run longer durations, decreasing your CP/FTP accordingly. Graphically, looking back at the CP chart, the vertical part of the hyperbolic curve will be steeper, leading to the horizontal part being flatter and the power level that the horizontal end of the hyperbolic curve approaches but never meets being at a lower intensity – a lower CP/FTP.

A third reason your CP/FTP has decreased depends on which CP/FTP calculation you're using.

If you're using CP testing, your CP/FTP may calculate lower if you over-performed the short test (compared to the long test) or under-performed the long test (compared to the short test). Take a look at previous tests to see if this might be the case. If so (and you're sure it's not because you're detraining), you might consider scheduling another test a week or so later; alternatively, you can continue using your previous CP/FTP.

If, instead, you're using FTP or Auto-CP (which both use maximum efforts from multiple workouts), it's likely that a maximum effort has dropped out of the 90-day window that these calculations typically use. Both WKO (FTP) and the Stryd PowerCenter (Auto-CP) allow you to view Power-Duration curves for custom date ranges – you should examine your PD-Curve from before your CP/FTP decreased to identify which maximum effort dropped out of the 90-day window, and schedule a new maximum effort run to fill the gap.

Will a lower-intensity run affect my CP/FTP?

★ CP/FTP is calculated using maximum efforts, not lower intensity (sub-maximal) runs.

The calculation works by examining all runs in the last 90 days, but sub-maximal runs are very unlikely to include a maximum compared to other workouts in the 90-day window.

☺ If you notice that your CP/FTP *has* changed after a sub-maximal run, then it's very likely that the calculation doesn't have sufficient max effort runs, and you should run some maximal efforts to ensure your CP/FTP is valid.

How can I calculate my CP/FTP if I've not been training recently?

Maximum efforts can be challenging to execute well, especially if you've not been training recently or have an increased risk of injury.

In this case, you can use calculations based on easy runs to get a usable CP estimate that can be used until you've trained enough to attempt a maximum effort. You can use the "talk test" to confirm you're running at an easy intensity – while running, if you can hold a conversation without gasping for breath, you're running easy.

☺ You can estimate CP/FTP by multiplying the average power of three easy runs (the sections when you were running easy rather than warming up or cooling down) by 1.25. This method assumes that when you run easy, you're running at around 80% of your CP/FTP *[Palladino; A method to roughly estimate FTP/CP]*.

While this method provides a rough estimate that you can use to begin training, the estimate may be as much as 2-5% in error. You should schedule a CP test or 2-3 maximum effort runs of differing durations as soon as you're able, so you can train using a more accurate CP/FTP.

Multi-sport CP/FTP

Your running CP/FTP is unrelated to your cycling or swimming FTP, even if the numbers appear similar.

This is due to different sports using different muscles, differing limb movements, differing elastic energy contributions and differing power meters and power calculations.

★ If you are a multi-sport athlete, you should calculate CP/FTP separately for each sport.

Chapter 4

Workouts

What's coming up?

You have your watch and power meter and have purchased or subscribed to your supporting apps to plan and monitor your training. Is there anything you need to do before going for a run?

This chapter covers items you should consider before your first power-based workout to ensure your best in-run experience and that your workouts provide data supporting meaningful metrics without unexpected consequences.

Here's a summary of what the chapter covers ...

Most running watches aren't set up "out of the box" for Running with Power. You'll need to consider a few things so your watch is configured to Run with Power.

The first is what your watch shows when you're running. Since you'll be Running with Power, you'll want to see power, but should you choose real-time or average power? And what else might you want to see along with power?

Your height and weight are used when Running with Power, and changes to either will impact your power readings if you display them in Watts. You should not change your weight once it is set, and if you have smart scales or similar devices, you should remove any auto-update of your weight setting from your smart scales.

There are also a few configuration settings that can lead to unexpected results when running or unexpected results when reviewing.

Auto-lap is useful on easy or longer runs. It's less useful when running intervals, especially longer intervals – they may be split in your analysis tool when auto-lap is enabled.

Auto-pause or manually pausing your watch may result in overstated power averages. When training, this may lead you to conclude that you ran to your target range when, in fact, your intensity was too low and you've not met your workout goal. If your watch has it, you should turn off Auto-pause.

Auto-calibrate adjusts the way your watch measures speed and distance using GPS signals for the adjustment. But this will impact your Running Effectiveness (RE) measurement, which you will need when setting event targets. If your watch has it, you should turn off Auto-calibrate.

You don't have to follow the suggestions in this chapter, but if you do, you'll avoid frustrations and potential confusion later on. The last thing you want to experience is getting frustrated during a workout or confused when your completed workout data is inaccurate and impacting your metrics.

Your watch display

What's in this section?

Real-time power can be a little disconcerting and sometimes frustrating when an apparently random reading takes your power outside your target range and generates an alert on your watch.

You can use power averaging to smooth out real-time power.

If you use power averaging, select an averaging period appropriate to your workout structure (shorter averaging periods for interval sessions, longer for easy or long runs).

Interval sessions use laps to break a run into work and recovery sections. You can use lap power (the average power for a lap) along with current power to stay within your target range for your work sections.

You can use lap power to stay within your target range on longer runs by using auto-lap to break the longer run into shorter sections.

Previous lap power lets you check your work power while in the recovery lap.

Take some time to consider what you want to display on your watch when running easy or long runs (with no defined intervals) compared to running higher-intensity interval runs.

Power averaging

Human power output is stochastic, appearing to vary randomly (but within a predictable pattern).

If you monitor the instant-by-instant (real-time) output from a running power meter, the values it displays will appear almost random, with one reading having little in common with the next.

Many power meter/watch combinations support real-time power. While this allows you to experience how jumpy power is while you run, it can be a little disconcerting and sometimes frustrating when a random reading takes your power outside your target range and generates an alert on your watch.

☺ Instead of real-time power, many runners use a 3-second or 10-second average when running. The average of the real-time power readings smooths the jumpiness and provides a more stable power reading.

However, going too far the other way is also possible, especially when running a workout with shorter intervals. For example, a 10-second average may not work very well when running 30-second repeats at 115-120% of CP/FTP, as it will take 10-15 seconds to show your work power and another 10-15 seconds to show your recovery power at the end of each interval.

★ In summary, if you choose to use power averaging, you should use an averaging period that's appropriate to your workout structure (shorter averaging periods for interval sessions, longer for easy or long runs).

Lap Power

When running intervals, your workout will typically be divided into work sections, where you aim to keep your average power (not your real-time power) within a target range, and recovery sections, where you give your body time to recover for the following work interval.

These will most likely use work and recovery laps on your watch, and many watches can be set up to show the average power for the current lap.

You can use lap power along with current power to stay within your target range for the current lap (after all, the aim is that your average power ends up within your target range, not your real-time power):

- Set up your watch display to show both lap power and current power.

- Run your current lap so that your average lap power and current power are within your target range.

- If your lap power goes above your target range, decrease your effort, using a current power below your target range to bring your lap power back into your target range.

- If your lap power goes below your target range, increase your effort, using a current power above your target range to bring your lap power back into your target range.

It sounds complicated, but it becomes easier after a few workouts.

☺ Using a method like this will also pay dividends on longer runs, where you can use auto-lap to break the longer run into shorter sections and use lap power to stay within your target range. This is especially useful when you are tired towards the end of the run.

Previous Lap Power

Previous lap power is also useful, as it lets you check your work power while in the recovery lap.

☺ This can be easier than continually monitoring your current lap power, as it means you can run your work laps without looking at your watch, using alerts to let you know when you're above or below your target range, then check the average power of your work lap while recovering ready for the next work lap.

This, in turn, enables you to practice running by perceived effort, training your ability to feel just how much effort you're using.

Your watch display

Running with Power is still reasonably new in the running community. Most recent watches arrive ready for running by pace or heart rate (HR), with no power metrics visible on your watch display.

Take some time to consider what you want to display when running easy or long runs (with no defined intervals) compared to running higher-intensity interval runs.

You may choose to display the same metrics for every run, or you may choose to use a longer power averaging for easy or long runs and a shorter power averaging for intervals. If your watch has running profiles, you can use them to set up different configurations.

You may choose a minimal display with two or three power metrics and no other metrics visible. You may also choose to show pace or HR along with power.

☺ There's no correct answer – you should set up your watch to show the metrics you want to monitor while running.

Personal experience and conversations in Facebook groups suggest that many runners work through something similar to the following:

1. Initially, power is unfamiliar. You have power showing on your watch, but you also have pace or HR as these are the metrics you're familiar with, and you can cross-check your intensity using a familiar metric while getting used to Running with Power. You run with five or more metrics visible on your watch, sometimes glancing at power, other times glancing at pace or HR.

2. After a while, you find that power doesn't always match your pace or HR, sometimes decreasing when the other metrics increase and sometimes increasing when the other metrics remain constant. It feels a little confusing, and you may be unsure what each metric tells you about your intensity and which metric you should use. It would be best if you decided which is your primary metric: you may choose to remain with pace/HR as your primary metric, relegating power to an "interesting but not for me" metric, or you may choose the opposite, making power your primary metric and relegating pace/HR. You might also adjust your setup to have a power screen and a pace/HR screen, switching between the data screens if necessary.

3. If you've chosen power as your primary metric, you might set up your power screen to show two or more power metrics plus additional metrics related to Running with Power – for example, Power Zone (covered in the **Training** chapter), Running Effectiveness (covered in the **Races & Events** chapter), or % of CP/FTP (covered in the **Training** Chapter). You may also add non-power metrics like cadence or Ground Contact Time to work on keeping those within acceptable limits. You still run with five or more metrics on your watch. While your primary focus is Running with Power (and keeping your power within workout targets), your focus is split between your running intensity (power)

and other metrics unrelated to running intensity.

4. Eventually, you might realise that less is more and that Running with Power is simply a way to train your ability to feel how hard you're running – to train your perceived exertion. You adjust your watch display to show two metrics (lap power and 3s/10s average power), adding previous lap power when running intervals. You may also include total elapsed time, the current time of day to keep track of the time, or total distance to keep track of how far you've run, although duration is often the better choice when Running with Power and using Power-Duration targets.

The above sequence is not unusual and may even be necessary to become entirely comfortable with Running with Power.

Height & Weight settings

What's in this section?

Keep your weight setting fixed, and don't change it to reflect changes in your weight.

Disconnect any services feeding your day-to-day weight into your power meter so that your weight setting is not automatically updated.

If you're measuring CP/FTP in Watts, changing your weight setting may invalidate your CP/FTP, all metrics based on your CP/FTP and any other metrics that use weight in their calculation.

There are a few scenarios where you may choose to change your weight setting (see below for when you might consider this).

Why do power meters need height and weight?

Power measures effort. It takes more effort to move a heavier body. If you run into a headwind, it takes more effort to overcome the headwind with a bigger body than a smaller one. This is why power meters ask for your weight and height when you set them up.

Once entered, your height is unlikely to change, but your weight fluctuates daily (even hourly) – not by much, but it does fluctuate. Over days or weeks, your weight can increase or decrease significantly.

If your weight changes, should you update your weight setting so that your power readings reflect those changes?

☺ Keep your weight fixed, and *don't* change it to reflect changes in your weight. Furthermore, if you use intelligent scales or other devices that make your weight available to online services, disconnect any services feeding your day-to-day weight into your power meter so that your weight is not automatically updated.

Why should you keep your weight fixed?

When power meters calculate your power, the result is in Watts/kg – the effort needed to move 1 kilogram. But most watches and supporting apps work in Watts, not Watts/kg. Your power meter or watch multiplies the result in Watts/kg by the weight you've configured (in kg) to display a final result in Watts. Your weight is being used as a conversion factor.

The issue with weight changes becomes apparent when you want to calculate power metrics that use values from multiple workouts.

Here's an analogy using coins, currencies, and conversion factors.

Imagine that each workout you do produces a coin representing its value. The coin is in a specific currency, determined by your weight setting, and the coins are extra shiny if your workout is a max effort. Over time, you'll have a pile of coins, each of a different value. If you keep your weight setting unchanged, all the coins will be in the same currency. If you change your weight setting, your pile will contain coins of differing currencies.

Now, imagine you want to calculate Auto-CP or FTP. You pick out the extra shiny max efforts and run the values through the multi-parameter model to calculate your current CP/FTP. What currency is the result in? If you've kept your weight constant, the result will be in the same currency as your coins. But if you've adjusted your weight, you won't be able to determine the currency – sure, you can get a number, but it's like adding Euros to Dollars to Pounds ... the result is meaningless *unless* you convert the coins to a common currency first. As most running websites use Watts and don't do any conversion to Watts/kg, it's best to avoid the issue in the first place by keeping your weight fixed.

The same happens if you want to calculate Stress Balances to monitor your training load, although this time, you use all the coins, not just the shiny ones. Because Stress Balances use values from multiple workouts, you have the same issue. If the coins are in differing currencies (because your weight setting was changed), you can get a numeric result, but the number is meaningless *unless* you convert the coins to a common currency first. Stress Balances (TSB and RSB) are covered in the **Training** chapter.

This is why cyclists use Watts/kg (not Watts), avoiding the conversion issue as all workout values are already Watts/kg.

The impact of changing your weight

Changing your weight impacts more than just the number shown by your power meter:

- Your CP/FTP combines results from multiple runs. If each run uses a different weight setting, your CP/FTP will be calculated using different conversion factors and will no longer be valid. It's like calculating a total using amounts in different currencies – you can add up the numbers, but the result is meaningless because it combines different currencies.

- Worse, everything that uses your CP/FTP will also be invalid – workout targets, stress scores, training load metrics, and even race-day goals.

- Your weight may also be used to calculate other metrics specific to your power meter, like Leg Spring Stiffness (a Stryd metric). In this case, changing your weight will also impact the calculation of LSS and will mean you can no longer track this metric over time.

★ In summary, keep your weight setting fixed when using Watts (or other measures not normalised to 1kg).

Won't my power values be invalid if my actual weight has changed?

No.

Power meters calculate power in Watts/kg, as shown by the following formulae:

Power = Force * Speed
Force = Mass * Acceleration

... therefore...

Power = Mass * Acceleration * Speed
Power/Mass = Acceleration * Speed

As speed is related to acceleration, all you need to calculate power (in Watts/kg) is an accelerometer (or multiple accelerometers set perpendicular to each other) and a model.

★ Regardless of your actual weight or the weight setting in your power meter, the Watts/kg number will *always reflect your actual effort*.

Should you ever change your weight?

There are a few scenarios where you might choose to change your power meter weight:

- Your weight has changed significantly (by more than 3kg), *and* you're beginning a new training block. During the training block, you'll be using results from multiple workouts for CP/FTP and other metrics, so it's essential that your weight setting remains unchanged. At the start of a new block, you can make a one-time change, but note that this will mean you'll need to reset your CP/FTP as if you'd just started Running with Power. Your previous CP/FTP and results from previous training cycles won't be able to be directly compared to the results in your new training cycle – to compare them, you'll need to convert to a common weight (or currency) first.

- You're running in different environmental conditions than usual and want to include the workout in your training metrics for the current training cycle. More on this later (see the **Environments** chapter), but changing your weight can be used to compensate for changes in heat, humidity, or altitude (for example, when running on a treadmill compared to running outside).

- You're running with extra weight, such as a backpack. This can create a mismatch between your workout targets and your actual power numbers for the workout, as you'll be working at a higher intensity than your watch shows. To compensate, you could manually change your weight setting so that your CP/FTP and workout targets remain unchanged while your power numbers will better match the effort taken to produce them.

- You track all metrics using values normalised to 1 kg. In this case, your weight doesn't matter, as you're using Watts/kg rather than Watts and kN/m/kg rather than kN/m for Leg Spring Stiffness. You can update your weight as often as you like and connect your power meter to your smart scales or other devices tracking your general health metrics.

Other watch settings

What's in this section?

You can use lap power to stay within your target range on longer runs by using auto-lap to break the longer run into shorter sections.

For interval runs, it's better not to have auto-lap active so that you can monitor the lap average over the entire work interval.

To ensure the data you use to analyse your runs is based on actual effort over actual durations, use elapsed time (not moving time), turn off the auto-pause feature on your watch, and don't manually pause it at any time. Of course, you can pause your running if you need to (just don't pause your watch)!

Auto-lap

Some watches have an auto-lap feature that allows you to move to the next lap after a set time or distance.

This can be useful for easy runs or long runs where the majority of the run is completed at one intensity, as it breaks the run into manageable sections and enables you to check whether each section is within the expected target range without having to break the run into sections when planning it.

But auto-lap can get in the way when running intervals – especially when the work interval duration is longer than the auto-lap duration. Your watch may switch to a new lap partway through the planned duration, leaving you guessing whether the entire interval was within target.

★ In summary, it's better not to have auto-lap active when running an interval workout so that you can monitor the lap average over the entire work interval.

☺ One way to achieve this, which means you don't have to keep adjusting your watch setup, is to use run profiles if your watch has them. Set up a run profile for easy or long runs with auto-lap enabled. Set up a copy of the run profile (or use one of the other pre-configured run profiles) for interval workouts, and turn off auto-lap.

Auto-pause (or manually pausing your watch)

Some watches have an auto-pause feature that can pause your watch if you drop below a certain speed (for example, if you stop at an intersection waiting to cross the road). You might also use watch buttons to pause your workout manually.

☺ You might think that pausing your workout when you're not running is the right thing to do so that your workout stats exclude non-workout time. However, when Running with Power, this will lead to inaccurate power averages compared to your target ranges, and you may miss achieving your training goals.

How?

Imagine you want to run a 10-minute interval with a power target of 240W. You run it one day on a route with no stops. Your power average is 240W whether you use moving time or elapsed time since your watch recorded you moving for the entire 10 minutes.

Now imagine the same 10-minute interval (at 240W), with 5 minutes waiting for a train to clear a level crossing (wishing you hadn't chosen a route that crossed a train line!). If you calculate power averages using moving time, with your watch paused while you stand around, your average power will be 240W. But if you calculate using elapsed time, your average power will be 240W * 10 min / 15 min = 160W.

Which is a better match to your effort over the interval? The calculation using elapsed time is better since it includes your effort over the entire interval duration, and you were standing around for 5 minutes with no effort involved.

The impact? Pausing your watch may lead you to conclude that you ran to your target range when, in fact, your intensity was too low, and you missed achieving your training goals.

★ In summary, when Running with Power, you should use elapsed durations (not moving time), turn off auto-pause on your watch and not manually pause your workout at any time.

Auto-calibrate

Auto-calibrate adjusts the way your watch measures speed and distance using GPS signals for the adjustment. This is a convenience function, using GPS as a reference to improve the accuracy with which your watch reports distance and the pace at which you're running.

But what does pace have to do with power? Isn't power about effort and duration (not distance or pace)?

Power *is* about effort and duration. But recalibrating your watch (whether manually or automatically) will impact your Running Effectiveness (RE) – how effectively you convert power into speed.

RE is used for several things: to track improvements over time, estimate an event finish time, monitor the impact of working on your form, and compare runners or running shoes.

However, RE calculated under one calibration will give a different result if calculated using a different calibration, as calibration is being used as a conversion or scaling factor (similar to how your weight is used to display power numbers in Watts – see the Height & Weight section in this chapter for more on this).

If your calibration is changed, you won't be able to track improvements over time or monitor the impact of working on your form, and critically, you may not have reliable RE numbers with which to set event targets.

Of course, you may consciously choose to change your calibration if it's wrong. But consciously choosing can be done between training blocks and is very different than having your calibration changed on an ongoing basis, perhaps even without you knowing the change was made.

★ In summary, if your watch has it, you should turn off Auto-calibrate.

Chapter 5

Training

What's coming up?

Training is a balance. Your workouts stress your body, providing a stimulus for your body to adapt (with the aim of improving performance), but that stress also creates fatigue. In addition, the adaptations need time to develop – time for "the magic to happen".

How does Running with Power help you achieve the right balance between adaptation and fatigue?

Here's a summary of what the chapter covers ...

There are a few models describing how your body adapts to exercise:

- The Stimulus-Fatigue-Recovery-Adaptation (SFRA) model, often called the super-compensation model, is based on how repeated bouts of exercise appeared to build compensation on compensation (or adaptation on adaptation).

- The Impulse-Response model recognises that training causes two separate types of responses, one shorter-term and another longer-term, but uses quite complex calculations and is based on heart rate.
- More recent work by Andrew Coggan, PhD, has extended the Impulse-Response model to create the Performance Manager model, which is based on power and uses metrics that can be calculated outside of a laboratory setting.

This chapter briefly describes the earlier models and then focuses on the Performance Manager model. It covers the model as presented in *[Allen, Coggan & McGregor; Performance Manager]*, including sections on each of the Performance Manager Metrics – Training Stress Scores (TSS), Chronic Training Load (CTL), Acute Training Load (ATL) and Training Stress Balance (TSB)

It also covers the more recent Stryd model (which is based on the Performance Manager model) and the equivalent Stryd metrics – Running Stress Scores (RSS) and Running Stress Balance (RSB).

You don't need to know the Performance Manager *and* the Stryd model, as your choice of model (and metrics) will probably be based on your choice of equipment and apps. The metrics in both models enable you to *monitor your training load* and the *balance between fatigue and adaptation*.

The metrics sections conclude with Ramp Rate (which enables you to track how quickly you add or remove training stress) and Training Intensity Distribution (which enables you to monitor the mix of intensities in your training to ensure that it is appropriate for *your goal event*).

The metrics used to monitor your training can *also* be used to plan your training load and mix of intensities. This will allow you to plan the training progression that will get the most from your training while keeping your injury risk low – the planning section covers how to do that.

Whether you create your own training plan or buy a training plan, training progression is essential. This (and other criteria) are covered in the section on choosing a training plan.

Training is reversible. The effect of reducing or stopping your training (detraining) is the same whether you train by power, heart rate or pace. What is different is the impact on your power metrics, which are quick to show performance gains but slow to show performance declines. The final section covers these impacts and how to handle them.

The terms used in this section

This section is the largest in the book and introduces several new terms (on top of the training metric acronyms), some of which are very similar. The following should help you understand the terms:

- Stimulus, Impulse and Stress. Running stresses your body. That stress pushes your body to adapt, providing a training stimulus or training impulse (the two are equivalent). I use the terms stimulus and impulse in the next section (explaining different adaptation models) but then use stress throughout the rest of the chapter.

- **Training load** and Ramp Rate. Training load refers to accumulated training stress. It's the load you've placed on your body via repeated training bouts. If you increase your training load too quickly (if your ramp rate is too high), you'll increase your risk of injury.

- **Training progression**. Training isn't just repeating the same workouts repeatedly – if you do that, you'll eventually reach a plateau where your workouts aren't challenging your body. If instead you gradually increase your training volume, perhaps by increasing the duration of your long runs, adding extra intervals or reducing your recovery time between intervals, you'll provide the training stress your body needs to continue to adapt – you'll be progressing your training.

What happens when you train?

> Stimulus-Fatigue-Recovery-Adaptation

F=Fatigue
R=Recovery
A=Adaptation

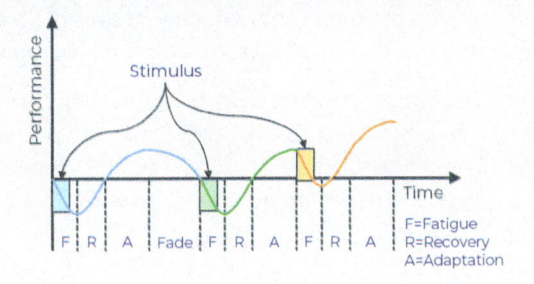

What's in this section?

The Stimulus-Fatigue-Recovery-Adaptation (SFRA) model attempted to explain what happens when you exercise, but it's been found to be a simplified model.

The Impulse-Response model better explains what happens when you exercise. It recognises that a single training impulse creates shorter-term fatigue and longer-term adaptation, with both occurring simultaneously.

The Performance Manager model enables the Impulse-Response model to be used with power and applied outside a laboratory setting.

★ Stress Scores from completed workouts can be used to calculate shorter-term, and longer-term moving averages. The two combine to give a

Stress Balance, indicating whether you are training with a "productive" training balance and when you may be in danger of over-training.

Changes in the longer-term moving average can be used to monitor how quickly training Stress accumulates (a Ramp Rate), reducing injury risk.

Your Training Intensity Distribution (TID) can be used to plan and track the mix of training intensities appropriate for your goal event and appropriate for where you are in your training plan.

The Stimulus-Fatigue-Recovery-Adaptation model

Your body is a wonderful thing. If you ask it to do something new, the first time may be difficult, and if you push it too far, you may suffer aches and pains and need a few days to recover. But try the same thing again (once recovered), and your body seems more able to do what you're asking it to do, with less recovery needed afterwards. Eventually, if you keep at it, you may find that you can achieve whatever you're attempting with minimal (if any) recovery – your body has adapted.

Simply put, you've applied a training stimulus, and your body has adapted. Of course, it's not as simple as "training 'in', adaptation and improved performance 'out'".

The chart at the beginning of this section shows the Stimulus-Fatigue-Recovery-Adaptation (SFRA) model proposed by *[Rowbottom; SFRA model]*: Apply a training Stimulus, and your body responds by becoming Fatigued. But give it time to Recover, and it Adapts. If you don't apply further training Stimulus, the Adaptation fades (the first cycle in the chart). But if you apply a further Stimulus, and then at the point where your body is Adapting you apply a further Stimulus, the Adaptations start accumulating.

This model is also known as the supercompensation model (based on how repeated bouts of exercise appear to build adaptation on adaptation – compensation on compensation). While it goes some way to explaining what happens when you train, it has some shortcomings:

- It's challenging to identify how long to allow for Recovery and Adaptation before applying another training Stimulus. Do it too soon, and you'll layer Fatigue on Fatigue – the cumulative effect will be performance reductions. Do it too late, and your adaptation may already be fading – you'll have missed out on potential accumulated performance gains.

- It encourages you to think that you need to train, then rest, then train, then rest, to allow time for the adaptations. In reality, the training Stimulus will already have triggered your body to Adapt – there's no need to rest after *every* training Stimulus.

- The model has no numbers – it's difficult to quantify the impact of your training Stimuli so that you can understand whether you're training too much or too little.

The Impulse-Response model

In fact, two things are happening in parallel to give rise to the chart at the beginning of this section, and a formal model was proposed by *[Banister; Impulse-Response Model]* with the following characteristics:

- Training acting as "input".
- A change in predicted performance as the "output".
- Negative shorter-term consequences from recent workouts (fatigue, aches, pains).
- Positive longer-term adaptations that can result in performance improvements.

★ The positives and negatives combine, with the negative consequences dominating in the shorter term (producing the "fatigue dip") and the positive adaptations dominating in the longer term (producing the "super-compensation adaptation").

According to *[Allen, Coggan & McGregor; Impulse-Response Model]*, "the factors that the *[Banister; Impulse-Response Model]* takes into account have been shown to account for more than 70%, and often more than 90%, of the day-to-day variation in performance."

The most widely used metric to track an individual workout's impact on training load using the

Impulse-Response model is Banister's heart rate-based "training impulse" (TRIMP) score.

But rather than mix heart-rate training and power-based training, is there a power-based equivalent?

The Performance Manager model

[Allen, Coggan & McGregor; Performance Manager] proposes a power-based equivalent that works "in a manner consistent with the results of previous scientific research yet is still simple enough to be used and applied outside of a laboratory setting", with the following components:

- A Training Stress Score (TSS) calculated for each workout based on volume *and* intensity. TSS is a numeric score representing the relative stress of each workout.

- A Chronic Training Load (CTL) that uses TSS scores to model the longer-term (chronic) improvements from your training – a relative indicator of *changes in your performance ability due to training stress to which your body may have adapted*.

- An Acute Training Load (ATL) that uses TSS scores to model the shorter-term (acute) impacts of your training – a relative indicator of *changes in your performance ability due to training stress to which your body has not yet adapted*.

- A Training Stress Balance (TSB) that tracks the difference between your CTL and ATL. A positive TSB indicates your training may be too easy, a slightly negative TSB indicates a "productive" training balance, and a very negative TSB may indicate you're at risk of over-training or injury.

The performance manager model:

- recognises that a single training stimulus has shorter-term and longer-term impacts, both driven by the stress of the workout
- models training load based on workout stress (the greater the stress, the higher the load)
- accumulates training load, showing the result as an ongoing balance between shorter-term negative impacts and longer-term positive adaptations
- provides numbers that can be used to quantify the stress from workouts of differing intensity and duration, numbers that can be used (along with how you feel) to gauge whether you're training too much or too little, and to plan upcoming training balance

Stryd's training metrics

The Stryd PowerCenter presents a similar approach to the performance manager model:

- A Running Stress Score (RSS) calculated for each workout based on volume *and* intensity.
- A 42-day weighted average that uses RSS scores to model the longer-term impacts of your training.
- A 7-day weighted average that uses RSS scores to model the shorter-term impacts of your training.
- A Running Stress Balance (RSB) that tracks the difference between your 42-day and 7-day weighted averages.

RSS is calculated differently than TSS, "the difference coming from the fact that the equation for RSS is intended to account for the additional biomechanical stress put on your body from running" [*Stryd: How RSS differs from TSS*]. However, once you input each into their respective training load models, the difference between RSS and TSS is minor.

Training Intensity Distribution

The Performance Manager model and Stryd's Running Stress Balance aren't the whole picture regarding training, as they're based on Stress Scores, which combine Volume and Intensity. This means it's possible to get the same Stress Score from a longer, slower run and a shorter, more intense run, yet the stimulus and adaptations from these two runs are different.

Your Training Intensity Distribution (TID) charts the mix of intensities in your training. It's typically shown as weekly percentage bars that split your range of intensities into "zones" and show the percentage of time you spent (or plan to spend) training in each zone.

Your TID enables you to target and track the mix of intensities appropriate to the adaptations that will be most beneficial for your target event.

Training Stress Score (TSS)

What's in this section?

TSS represents the metabolic stress of a workout relative to your FTP (your individual metabolic fitness) and relative to other workouts.

TSS combines intensity and duration – harder *or* longer activities lead to higher scores.

TSS can be calculated for completed workouts (based on actual intensities and durations) and planned workouts (based on planned intensities and durations).

What is it?

TSS is a score that represents the metabolic stress of individual workouts relative to your FTP (your individual metabolic fitness). It's based on intensity and duration, with harder *or* longer activities leading to higher scores.

Why is it needed?

So that you can quantify the relative stress of each workout and use the numbers as the input for modelling training load accumulation or modelling planned training load.

The *[Allen, Coggan & McGregor; Performance Manager]* concept models the impacts of each workout's training stress. To do that, the model needs numbers representing each workout's stress.

TSS provides a score for each workout, representing the metabolic stress of each workout relative to other workouts and your FTP. In other words:

- longer or harder workouts have a higher score than shorter or easier workouts
- if our FTPs are different, your TSS for a specific workout will be different to my TSS for the same workout – TSS is relative to FTP, and FTP is a measure of *individual* metabolic fitness.
- if your FTP is inaccurate, your TSS will also be inaccurate

How to measure or calculate it?

It's calculated from a workout's Normalised Power (NP), its Intensity Factor (the workout's intensity compared to FTP), its duration, and your FTP.

The calculation is detailed in [*Allen, Coggan & McGregor; Training Stress Score*].

The TSS calculation produces a score of 100 for a 1-hour workout at FTP. This is the same for every runner and acts as a baseline against which TSS scores from your workouts can be compared or combined.

How to use it?

TSS can be used:

- to quantify the relative stress of specific workouts, enabling the potential (and actual) stress from different workout types to be compared

- as the input for modelling training load accumulation, combining scores from a range of days or weeks to model your Chronic Training Load (CTL) and Acute Training Load (ATL) – the next section covers CTL and ATL

- as the basis for modelling planned training load by calculating TSS based on planned intensities and durations

Chronic Training Load (CTL) and Acute Training Load (ATL)

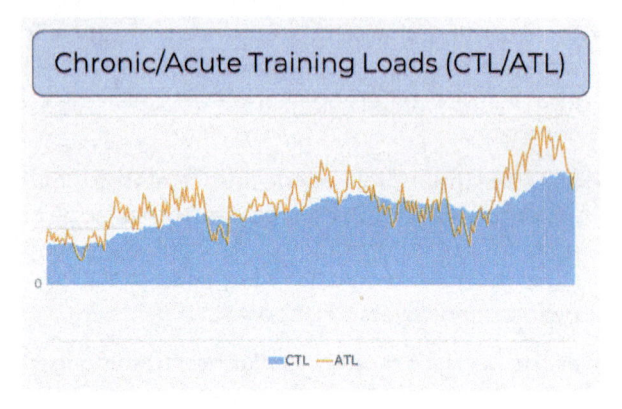

Chronic/Acute Training Loads (CTL/ATL)

What's in this section?

CTL and ATL are calculated using the training stress scores (TSS) from each of your workouts.

CTL models the longer-term positive impacts of your workouts – the changes in your performance ability due to training stress to which your body may have adapted.

ATL models the shorter-term negative impacts of your workouts – the changes in your performance ability due to training stress to which your body has not yet adapted.

CTL and ATL aren't usually monitored directly; they are intermediary metrics used to calculate your Training Stress Balance (TSB) and your Ramp Rate – metrics you should be monitoring.

CTL and ATL have been mislabelled "fitness" and "fatigue." They are not your fitness or fatigue; they're sport-specific relative indicators that must be interpreted within the context of overall fitness and fatigue.

What are they?

Your Chronic Training Load (**CTL**) models the longer-term (chronic) improvements from your training. CTL considers the last three months of workouts, with more recent workouts contributing more than older workouts. It's a relative indicator of changes in your performance ability due to changes in your fitness. In simple terms, CTL represents *changes in your performance ability due to training stress to which your body may have adapted*.

Your Acute Training Load (**ATL**) models the shorter-term (acute) impacts of your training. ATL considers the last two weeks of workouts, with more recent workouts contributing more than older workouts. It's a relative indicator of changes in your performance ability due to fatigue. In simple terms, ATL represents *changes in performance ability due to training stress to which your body has not yet adapted*.

Note: CTL and ATL are models, and as such, they are useful representations of reality, but they are NOT reality – they need to be interpreted appropriately.

Why are they needed?

So that you can model the shorter-term and longer-term impacts of training stress and use the numbers as the input for modelling training load accumulation or to model planned training load.

CTL and ATL are used to calculate your Training Stress Balance (TSB), which is covered in the next section. They are part of the *[Allen, Coggan & McGregor; Performance Manager]* model.

How to measure or calculate them?

CTL and ATL are calculated using the training stress scores (TSS) from each of your workouts.

They are calculated using an exponentially weighted moving average, with a shorter time constant for ATL (usually 7 days) and a longer time constant for CTL (usually 42 days).

The differing time constants reflect the different timescales over which shorter-term fatigue and longer-term adaptation affect your body.

How to use them?

CTL and ATL are intermediary metrics used to calculate:

- your Training Stress Balance (TSB) – covered in the next section

- your Ramp Rate – covered later in this chapter

Why not call CTL/ATL fitness and fatigue?

The Performance Manager model has been used as the basis for many implementations, many of which have not been approved by the model's originators. Worse, the original terms have been changed to be more runner-friendly, with CTL mislabelled as "fitness" and ATL mislabelled as "fatigue".

CTL and ATL are relative measures of fitness and fatigue rather than *actual* measures of your fitness and fatigue.

For example, imagine a scenario where, as a runner, you also swim and ride – yes, you're a triathlete. Because your sports use different muscle groups and power meters, you will have three different FTP values – one for each of the three sports (they can't be combined). When you complete a sport-specific workout, the TSS will be relative to that sport's FTP – TSS values can't be combined either. You'll have three different measures of Training Stress Balance, with differing CTL and ATL values underpinning TSB.

What is your actual fitness? Is it your running CTL, your swimming CTL or your cycling CTL? Or is it none of these since your overall fitness is some combination of the three? And what does overall fitness mean in this context? It's not a usable number since the sports are largely independent of each other. Plus, you may have other activities that should be considered (e.g. strength training).

Similar arguments can be made for ATL – it's not a measure of your actual fatigue, which will depend not only on training stress but also on sleep, nutrition, hydration, and stresses from other parts of your life (to name just a few).

★ Labelling these metrics fitness and fatigue is misleading – CTL and ATL are relative, sport-specific indicators and must be interpreted within the context of your overall fitness/fatigue.

Training Stress Balance (TSB)

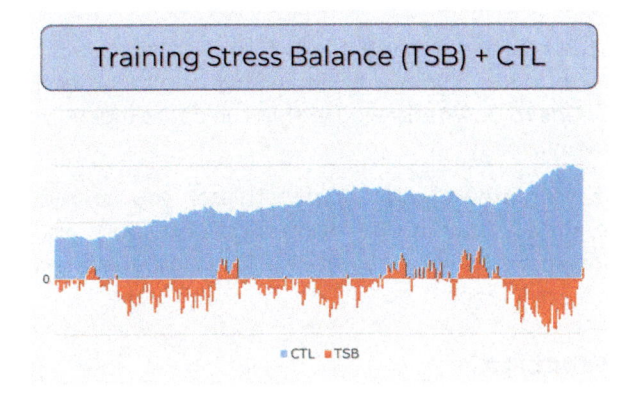

What's in this section?

TSB combines CTL and ATL to provide a stress balance.

A positive TSB indicates your training may be too easy, a slightly negative TSB indicates "productive" training balance and a very negative TSB may indicate you're at risk of over-training or injury.

TSB can be used to monitor the training load from completed workouts and to plan the training load for upcoming workouts.

You should track your TSB scores and compare them with how you feel as a result of your training so that you build your experience of TSB scores as they apply to you.

You need at least 60 days of TSS scores for TSB to be marginally useful and 80+ days of TSS scores for

TSB to be valid. Before those times, TSB scores are likely to give more negative results.

TSB has been mislabelled "form" – it's not your form; it's a sport-specific relative indicator that needs to be interpreted within the context of your overall form.

If you are a multi-sport athlete, you should maintain training load metrics per sport and interpret the mix of sport-specific numbers based on experience.

What is it?

Your Training Stress Balance (**TSB**) tracks the difference between your Chronic Training Load (CTL) and Acute Training Load (ATL).

A positive TSB indicates your training may be too easy, a slightly negative TSB indicates "productive" training balance and a very negative TSB may indicate you're at risk of over-training or injury.

Why is it needed?

So that you can

So that you can model training load accumulation and planned training load to reduce injury risk and plan a taper leading up to your event.

TSB combines the shorter-term impacts of training stress represented by ATL with the longer-term effects of training stress represented by CTL to give a "training balance".

TSB is a part of the [*Allen, Coggan & McGregor; Performance Manager*] model.

How to measure or calculate it?

The calculation is straightforward: TSB = CTL − ATL

How to use it?

TSB can be used to:

- model the impact of completed workouts using CTL/ATL calculated from actual training stress scores (TSS) – CTL and ATL are covered in the previous section
- plan upcoming workouts (to reduce the risk of overload) using CTL/ATL calculated from planned stress scores
- plan a taper (to arrive at the start fresh and ready to go) using CTL/ATL calculated from planned stress scores and a forward look based on your current TSB

☺ TSB scores, *as they apply to you as an individual*, need interpretation – there are no generally applicable ranges that include every individual. You should track your TSB and compare it with how you feel as a result of your training to build your experience of TSB as it applies to you.

★ The time constants used to calculate TSB from CTL/ATL mean that you need at least 60 days of TSS scores for TSB to be marginally useful and 80+ days of TSS scores for TSB to be valid. Before those times, TSB scores are likely to give more negative results.

Why not call TSB your form?

The Performance Manager model has been used as the basis for many implementations, many of which have not been approved by the model's originators. Worse, the original terms have been changed to be more runner-friendly, with TSB being mislabelled as "form".

TSB is based on CTL and ATL, which are relative measures of fitness and fatigue rather than actual measures of your fitness and fatigue.

For example, imagine a scenario where, as a runner, you also swim and ride – yes, you're a triathlete. Because your sports use different muscle groups and power meters, you will have three different FTP values – one for each of the three sports (they can't be combined). When you complete a sport-specific workout, the TSS will be relative to that sport's FTP – TSS values can't be combined either. You'll have three different measures of Training Stress Balance, with differing CTL and ATL values underpinning TSB.

What is your actual fitness? Is it your running CTL, your swimming CTL or your cycling CTL? Or is it none of these since your overall fitness is some combination of the three? And what does overall fitness mean in this context? It's not a usable number since the sports are largely independent of each other. Plus, you may have other activities that should be considered (e.g. strength training).

Similar arguments can be made for ATL – it's not a measure of your actual fatigue, which will depend not only on training stress but also on sleep, nutrition, hydration, and stresses from other parts of your life (to name just a few).

If CTL and ATL do not measure an athlete's actual fitness and fatigue, then TSB cannot measure an athlete's actual form.

★ Labelling this metric form is misleading – TSB is a relative, sport-specific indicator and needs to be interpreted within the context of your overall fitness/fatigue and form.

How does TSB work for multi-sports?

It's not designed to!

TSB is based on CTL and ATL, which are based on TSS calculations relative to FTP, and both TSS and FTP are based on power readings specific to individual sports and power meters.

★ Multi-sport athletes should maintain training load metrics per sport and interpret the mix of sport-specific numbers based on experience.

Running Stress Score (RSS)

What's in this section?

RSS is a Stryd innovation, roughly equivalent to TSS – if you use the Stryd ecosystem, you'll probably use RSS rather than TSS

RSS includes a coefficient that means your RSS scores differ from TSS scores for the same workouts. However, once you input each into their respective training load models, the difference between RSS and TSS is minor.

RSS represents the metabolic stress from a workout relative to your CP or Auto-CP (your individual metabolic fitness) and relative to other workouts.

RSS combines intensity and duration – harder *or* longer activities lead to higher scores.

RSS can be calculated for completed workouts (based on actual intensities and durations) and planned workouts (based on planned intensities and durations).

What is it?

RSS is a Stryd innovation, roughly equivalent to TSS

RSS is a score that represents the metabolic stress of individual workouts relative to your CP or Auto-CP (your individual metabolic fitness). It's based on intensity and duration, with harder *or* longer activities leading to higher scores.

Why is it needed?

So that you can quantify the relative stress of each workout and use the numbers as the input for modelling training load accumulation or to model planned training load.

Stryd's Running Stress Balance models the impacts of the training stress coming from each workout. To do that, the model needs numbers representing the stress of each workout.

RSS provides a score for each workout, representing the metabolic stress of each workout relative to other workouts and your CP or Auto-CP. In other words:

- longer or harder workouts have a higher score than shorter or easier workouts

- if our CPs are different, your RSS for a specific workout will be different to my RSS for the same workout – RSS is relative to CP or Auto-CP (these are a measure of *individual* metabolic fitness).

- if your CP or Auto-CP is inaccurate, your RSS will also be inaccurate

How to measure or calculate it?

It's calculated from a workout's second-by-second power, your CP, and a coefficient K, summing the second-by-second numbers to arrive at RSS for the workout.

[[Stryd; Running Stress Score]](#) details the calculation.

RSS is calculated slightly differently than TSS. The coefficient K results in a non-linear relationship between relative intensity and metabolic stress consistent with human metabolism response to relative intensity. However, once you input each into their respective training load models, the difference between RSS and TSS is minor.

The RSS calculation produces a score of 100 for a 1-hour workout at CP. This is the same for every runner and acts as a baseline against which TSS scores from your workouts can be compared or combined.

How to use it?

If you use the Stryd ecosystem, you'll probably use RSS rather than TSS

RSS can be used:

- to understand the relative stress of specific workouts, enabling the potential (and actual) stress from different workout types to be compared

- as the input for modelling your Running Stress Balance (RSB), covered in the next section

- as the basis for modelling planned training load by calculating RSS based on planned intensities and durations

Running Stress Balance (RSB)

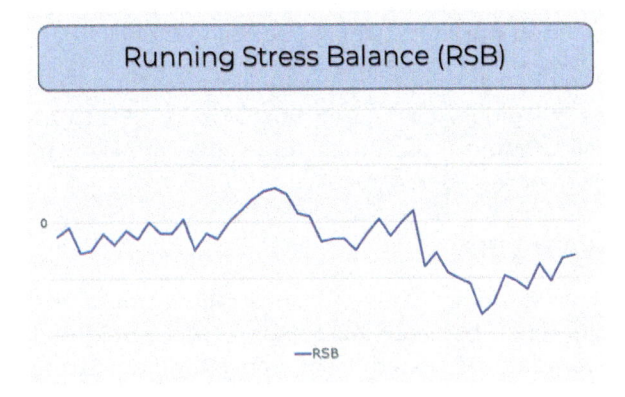

What's in this section?

RSB is a Stryd innovation, roughly equivalent to TSB – if you use the Stryd ecosystem, you'll probably use RSB rather than TSB

RSB combines 42-day and 7-day weighted averages of Running Stress Scores (RSS) to provide a Running Stress Balance (RSB).

The Stryd PowerCenter and mobile app provide an RSB score and an interpretation of that score, but the interpretation uses ranges that are likely to be population averages and may not be the best match for you and your ability.

You should track your RSB scores and compare them with how you feel as a result of your training so that you build your experience of RSB scores as they apply to you.

RSB can be used to monitor training load from completed workouts and can be estimated for planned workouts to plan upcoming training load.

You need at least 60 days of RSS scores for RSB to be marginally useful and 80+ days for RSB to be valid. Before those times, RSB scores are likely to give more negative results.

What is it?

Your Running Stress Balance (**RSB**) tracks the difference between 42-day and 7-day weighted averages calculated from your Running Stress Scores (RSS).

A positive RSB indicates your training may be too easy, a slightly negative RSB indicates "productive" training balance and a very negative RSB may indicate you're at risk of over-training or injury.

See *[Stryd: Running Stress Balance]* for a more detailed explanation.

Why is it needed?

So that you can model training load accumulation and planned training load to reduce injury risk and plan a taper leading up to your event.

RSB combines the shorter-term impacts of training stress, represented by your 7-day weighted average, with the longer-term effects of training stress, represented by your 42-day weighted average, to give a "training balance".

How to measure or calculate it?

The calculation is straightforward: RSB = 42-day weighted average – 7-day weighted average.

The weighted averages can be found in the *[Stryd; Mobile app]* by clicking the information indicator next to the RSB chart. They are calculated from your workout Running Stress Scores (RSS).

Note: The web-based [Stryd; PowerCenter] shows simple averages rather than exponentially weighted averages; RSB is, however, correctly calculated and displayed (using weighted averages).

How to use it?

RSB is used to model the impact of completed workouts, providing an RSB score and an interpretation of that score in the *[Stryd; Mobile app]* and the *[Stryd; PowerCenter]*.

☺ The ranges used by the descriptions (e.g. Productive is -25 to -5) most likely apply to a population of hundreds of athletes and may not apply to you as an individual. In other words, track your RSB yourself and compare it with how you feel as a result of your training so that you build your experience of RSB scores as they apply to you.

★ The time constants used to calculate RSB from the underlying weighted averages mean that you need at least 60 days of RSS scores for RSB to be marginally useful and 80+ days for RSB to be valid.

Before those times, RSB scores are likely to give more negative results.

While it's possible to calculate planned Running Stress Balance using RSS values for future workouts, the calculation would be manual and complex. This makes it difficult to plan based on future RSB, although it is possible to plan based on future RSS – on training load, not training load balance.

Ramp Rate

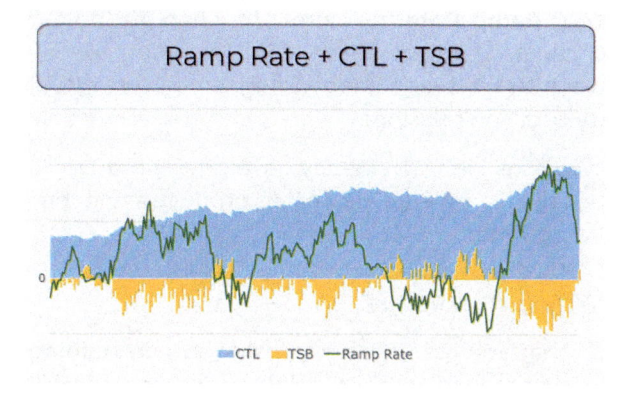

Ramp Rate + CTL + TSB

Note: The Ramp Rate in the above chart uses a different scale than CTL and TSB, so that changes in the rate can be seen more easily.

What's in this section?

Ramp Rate measures the changes in your training load – a positive rate indicates increasing load and a negative rate indicates decreasing load.

Ramp Rate can be calculated daily or weekly – calculating weekly removes daily peaks from long runs or high-intensity intervals.

Ramp Rate can be used to reduce injury risk, manage training load progression, and plan a taper.

What is it?

Your **Ramp Rate** measures the changes in your Chronic Training Load (CTL) or your 42-day weighted average (depending on which set of metrics you're using).

Increases in CTL/42-day average produce a positive Ramp Rate; decreases produce a negative Ramp Rate.

Why is it needed?

So that you assess how quickly you add training load to reduce your risk of injury, and how quickly you remove training load to plan a taper leading up to your event.

How to measure or calculate it?

To calculate your Ramp Rate, subtract the earlier CTL/42-day weighted average from the later CTL/42-day weighted average.

If you're using the Stryd 42-day average, ensure you use the value from the [*Stryd: Mobile app*], which shows a weighted average, rather than the value from the web-based [*Stryd: PowerCenter*], which shows a simple average.

Ramp Rates can be calculated daily (if you are actively training, your CTL/42-day weighted average will change daily).

They can also be calculated weekly as the difference between your CTL/42-day weighted average for two dates seven days apart (it is up to you to choose an appropriate day).

☺ Calculating weekly Ramp Rates removes daily peaks from long runs or high-intensity intervals.

How to use it?

Ramp Rate can be used to:

- avoid (or reduce the risk of) injury by keeping ramp rate values within a reasonable range – the range depending on your age and running history
- manage training load progression by maintaining a steady, runner-appropriate ramp rate progression
- plan a taper ready for an event by planning a negative ramp rate for the days before the event – the number of days depending on your CTL/42-day average, your age and the event type

Training Intensity Distribution

Training Intensity Distribution (TID)

Zone A Zone B Zone C

What's in this section?

Training Intensity Distribution (TID) tracks time spent at various intensities.

TID enables you to monitor your mix of intensities, ensuring it's appropriate for your goal event and training plan stage.

TID charts make use of training zones to group intensity ranges.

TID charts can show the percentage of time spent (the relative mix of intensities) or the total time spent (the overall intensity distribution).

What is it?

Your Training Intensity Distribution (**TID**) tracks time spent at various intensities so you can monitor the mix and adjust your upcoming intensity mix weekly or monthly.

Why is it needed?

So that you can monitor whether you're running at the mix of intensities appropriate for your goal event and your training plan stage.

Training Stress Balance (TSB) and Running Stress Balance (RSB) include intensity and duration, but neither allows insight into the composition or distribution of your training load.

TID provides insight into the composition and distribution of training intensity.

How to measure or calculate it?

It's as simple as analysing your runs to determine how much time you spent at each intensity.

But what does "each intensity" mean? To produce a usable chart, we need to group intensities; otherwise, we'd be looking at a chart with a gradually changing colour scheme and not be able to draw any useful conclusions.

Grouping intensities introduces the concept of Zones, which are explored more fully in the next section (the chart at the beginning of this section uses three zones).

We can produce a chart of time spent in each zone over the past few weeks. The chart can be organised in two different ways, to show:

- the percentage of total time spent in each zone – the relative mix of intensities
- the actual time spent in each zone – the intensity distribution within your training volume

Do you need to track this yourself? It depends on your reviewing app. Some apps include TID charts; others don't. If they do include TID charts, some allow you to use your choice of zones, and some don't. See the **Getting Started** chapter for more about choosing a reviewing app.

How to use it?

Training is not as simple as "if your goal race is a marathon, train at marathon intensities."

If you did that, your training would not stimulate the adaptations (to bones, tendons, and your cardiovascular system) that come from lower intensities, and you'd miss out on the adaptations that come from running at higher intensities. Many lower-intensity adaptations strengthen your body, reducing your risk of injury, and many higher-intensity adaptations improve your ability to produce energy and withstand fatigue.

Your TID enables you to monitor that your mix of intensities is appropriate for your goal event.

In addition, your mix of training intensities should progress. Earlier in the plan, you might focus on building a base with more time at lower intensities. Later, you might introduce more time at higher intensities to sharpen your running as you approach the event.

Your TID enables you to monitor that your mix of intensities is appropriate for your training plan stage.

Finally, when tapering, reducing volume while maintaining intensity is beneficial. This gives your body time to properly recover without losing your sharpness.

Your TID enables you to plan a mix of intensities appropriate for your taper.

Which training metrics should you use?

What's in this section?

TSS/TSB and RSS/RSB are similar approaches – both enable you to monitor your completed and planned training load.

Your choice of TSS/TSB or RSS/RSB will most likely depend on your choice of equipment and apps.

★ The three metrics you should monitor are TSB or RSB, Ramp Rate, and Training Intensity Distribution (TID) – the other training metrics are calculated in support of these three.

TSS/TSB and RSS/RSB are similar

★ If you've read the previous three sections, you've probably realised that Training Stress Scores/Training Stress Balance (TSS/TSB) and Running Stress Scores/Running Stress Balance (RSS/RSB) are very similar.

They:

- base their calculations on stress scores from individual workouts, combining volume *and* intensity
- model the shorter-term negative impacts and the longer-term positive impacts of training stress

- produce a number representing the current balance between negative and positive impacts that can be used to model your training load from completed workouts, plan training load from upcoming workouts and plan a taper

☺ You don't need to use both – the combination you choose to use will most likely depend on your choice of equipment and apps:

- If you use a *[Stryd; Footpod]* and the Stryd Ecosystem, you'll probably use RSS/RSB.

- If you purchased *[WKO]* or are training with a coach that uses TrainingPeaks, you'll probably use TSS/TSB.

- If you have neither, you'll probably use equivalents in whichever planning and reviewing apps you're using.

TSS/TSB and RSS/RSB are similar. That similarity extends to the weighted averages used within each system – Stryd's 42-day weighted average is similar to Chronic Training Load (CTL), and the 7-day weighted average is similar to Acute Training Load (ATL). The difference between the two is in the calculation of RSS vs. TSS.

Stryd does not offer a Ramp Rate, but you can calculate a weekly Ramp Rate by noting daily or weekly values for Stryd's 42-day weighted average.

Which metrics should I be monitoring?

- TSB/RSB. Your Training Stress Balance or Running Stress Balance indicates whether your training provides productive stress rather than too little or too much. The balances, *as they apply to you as an individual*, need interpretation – there are no generally applicable ranges that include every individual. You should track your TSB/RSB and compare it with how you feel as a result of your training to build your experience of TSB/RSB as it applies to you.

- Ramp Rate. Your Ramp Rate provides a perspective on your longer-term training load by calculating how quickly you add (or remove) load. It lets you minimise injury risk, manage your training load progression, and plan a taper.

- TID. Your Training Intensity Distribution (TID) provides insight into the composition and distribution of training intensity, allowing you to monitor whether you're running at the mix of intensities appropriate for your goal event and your training plan stage.

☺ While understanding the other metrics is helpful, they are calculated in support of the metrics above and don't need to be actively monitored.

Planning Training

What's in this section?

★ Different training intensities drive different physiological and performance adaptations.

Power enables your training to use precise target ranges (based on your CP/FTP) rather than less precise training zones.

Power enables training zones to be used when reviewing training (a descriptive use) rather than when setting training targets (a prescriptive use).

For most runners, it is wise to include recovery time to give your body time to deal with fatigue and adapt to the training stress – think of this as time "when the magic happens."

The power-based metrics used to monitor completed training can also be used to plan upcoming training.

Target zones vs. Target ranges

Different training intensities drive different physiological and performance adaptations [*Coggan; Cycling Power Zones*]. This is why most training plans contain runs a different intensities (some longer and slower, some shorter and faster.

When planning training, how do you decide which intensities to include?

The Fundamentals chapter introduced the concept of domains – medium through heavy, up into severe and extreme. While widely used by researchers, domains are too broad for planning training.

As a result, running coaches have introduced further divisions to create zones, with training zones available using heart rate, pace and power. Focusing on Running with Power (this is, after all, a book about that topic), power zone schemes are available from Garmin, Stryd, Vance, Fitzgerald, Palladino, Van Dijk and Van Megen, Dr. Will and many others.

But there is little agreement about where the zones should be divided – some have a division at or about CP/FTP, others have a single zone that straddles CP/FTP, and even with a single zone for CP/FTP, different schemes vary in how broad the zone is (95-105%? 98-102%?)

This leads to a few different questions, including one very important one.

Can zones be used to plan training?

If you're using a measure of intensity that is slow to respond to changes in effort or is affected by hills or wind, using wider zones may be a valuable way to target training. With wider zones, you can be confident that you'll be running at your target intensity at least some of the time. And if nothing else, using wider zones will reduce the number of alerts your watch gives you if you go above or below target!

Power is a little different in this respect, as it measures your effort and responds in real-time to changes in effort due to hills, wind, or similar factors. As long as you're using a power meter that is repeatable (same effort under same conditions = same power number) and valid (aligned to physiology), it is possible to use narrower target ranges within zones or domains.

☺ In summary, power enables more precise training targets and, as a result, allows training zones to be used descriptively rather than prescriptively – zones should be part of the review process, not part of the planning process.

Which zone scheme is best?

☺ In reviewing the available schemes, the one that makes the most sense to me, the one that seems best aligned to how our bodies work when running, is *[Palladino; Running Power Zones]*. But don't take my word for it – do your own research and settle on a zone scheme that works for you when you review your training intensities (using Training Intensity Distribution charts).

Mix of intensities

The Training Intensity Distribution (TID) section contains the following guidance on how to plan and monitor your mix of intensities using your TID.

Training is not as simple as "if your goal race is a marathon, train at marathon intensities."

If you did that, your training would not stimulate the adaptations (to bones, tendons, and your cardiovascular system) that come from lower intensities, and you'd miss out on the adaptations that come from running at higher intensities. Many lower-intensity adaptations strengthen your body, reducing your risk of injury, and many higher-intensity adaptations improve your ability to produce energy and withstand fatigue.

Your TID enables you to monitor that your mix of intensities is appropriate for your goal event.

In addition, your mix of training intensities should progress. Earlier in the plan, you might focus on building a base with more time at lower intensities. Later, you might introduce more time at higher intensities to sharpen your running as you approach the event.

Your TID enables you to monitor that your mix of intensities is appropriate for your training plan stage.

Finally, when tapering, reducing volume while maintaining intensity is beneficial. This gives your body time to properly recover without losing your sharpness.

Your TID enables you to plan a mix of intensities appropriate for your taper.

☺ If you're interested in how different training intensities drive different physiological and performance adaptations, a great place to start (even though it's focused on cycling rather than running) is *[Coggan; Cycling Power Zones]*.

Magic time

When planning training, it's wise to include time when you don't have any workouts.

Why?

Earlier in this chapter, we covered what happens when you train, which introduced the Stress-Fatigue-Recovery-Adaptation and the Impulse-Response models. Both models begin with training stress and conclude with how your body responds.

Your body responds in two different ways.

In the short term, the response is fatigue, perhaps aches or tightness. To reduce the risk of injury, it's wise to plan recovery time when you might focus on stretching or mobilisation (but not strength work) to manage the aches or tightness.

In the longer term, the response is (hopefully) adaptation. To support that adaptation and allow your body time to respond, it's also wise to plan recovery time when you might do something altogether different, giving your body and mind a break from training and returning to it feeling refreshed.

But there's another reason why you should plan recovery time.

Your body contains an autonomic nervous system (ANS) that functions without conscious control. It has two components – one that controls "fight-or-flight" responses and another that regulates "rest and digest" activity.

Running provides training stress, which activates your fight-or-flight nervous system. However, longer-term adaptations can only occur when your rest and digest nervous system is active – for which you must *not* be running.

★ It is wise to include recovery time in your training plan so that your body has time to deal with fatigue and so that your body can rest and digest the training stress.

And rather than thinking of it as wasted time, think of it as magic time... the time "when the magic happens" (a phrase I heard a while ago that speaks to the importance of recovery time).

Planned Training Load and Training Intensity Distribution

Use the metrics introduced in this chapter (TSS/CTL/ATL/TSB and RSS/RSB) to monitor your training load based on the actual durations and intensities of completed workouts.

You can also use them to plan training load based on planned workouts (and the planned durations and intensities within those workouts).

Some planning apps have these features built in. For example, *[TrainingPeaks; Training platform]* has planned and actual TSS by week in the calendar view, and the Dashboard view includes a performance manager chart showing CTL, ATL, and TSB.

Even if you choose a planning app that doesn't include these metrics, you can still calculate them manually.

The upcoming mix of intensities can also be planned using the intensities and durations of your upcoming workouts.

★ In summary, the metrics used to monitor completed training can also be used to plan upcoming training – to see the effect of adjusting workout durations or workout intensities, to plan a realistic training progression, to plan your intensity mix and to plan a taper leading up to an event.

Choosing a Training Plan

What's in this section?

Power-based training plans are different from plans based on heart rate or pace

☺ The criteria below can be used to evaluate a power-based training plan to ensure it fully supports Running with Power

Power-based training plans

The previous section described a few differences that you might expect to see in training plans based on power:

- Target ranges rather than target zones – power enables more precise training targets.

- Your mix of intensities – power metrics enables finer control over the intensities included in your plan.

- Training Stress for completed and planned workouts – the same metrics can be used when looking back and when looking ahead.

- Magic time – training load metrics remove the guesswork about recovery days or lighter weeks by enabling you to include appropriate recovery time in your plan.

Given these differences, you might expect power-based training plans to differ from plans you may have used before.

Some of them are different; some aren't.

While there are some common principles that every training plan should incorporate, there are some power-based principles that make power-based training plans different from pace- or heart rate-based plans.

How can you be sure that the power-based plan you're about to buy or embark on fully supports Running with Power?

Criteria for evaluating training plans

☺ Here are some criteria you could use to evaluate training plans, starting with criteria that could be applied to any plan and finishing with criteria that you should apply to plans that use power as their measure of intensity.

Any training plan should:

- be aligned to your goal event – the volume and intensity mix in a training plan for a marathon should be different than the mix in a plan for a 5k

- allow enough time for your body to adapt – the more adaptation needed (based on your current fitness and your target event), the longer the plan should be

- contain sufficient weekly workouts to provide the stimulus you need – plans should contain at least three runs each week

- contain different intensity workouts – running every workout easy or at a single intensity won't stimulate all of the adaptations your goal event may need

- progress workouts from week to week or section to section – progressing overall training volumes *and* volume at specific intensities (your volume is the time you spend training)

- allow time "for the magic to happen" – either as recovery between workouts, recovery days each week, by planning a lower volume every few weeks, or all three

- be structured to meet your recovery needs – a consideration for older runners or for runners that (for various reasons) may be more injury-prone

- be adaptable – no matter what you plan to do, "life happens", and your training plan should offer guidance about how to adjust your plan

- be "worth the money" – if you pay for a plan, you're more likely to look closely at the plan content and may be more likely to stick to the plan

In addition, power-based plans should:

- specify target intensities as percentages of CP/FTP – this aligns the plan to your power meter and individual metabolic fitness and builds in progression as your CP/FTP improves

- set higher-intensity interval targets based on CP/FTP and Reserve Work Capacity (RWC) – RWC varies from individual to individual and is a key metric for intensities above CP/FTP (it's covered in the **Power-Duration Curve** chapter)

- use target ranges rather than target zones – the use of target ranges is an indication that the plan was built to achieve specific adaptations through more targeted training stimuli

- include regular CP tests or max-effort runs – so that you maintain your CP/FTP as a built-in part of your training

- be geared to your current ability – your CP/FTP (expressed in Watts/kg) can be used to check that the plan is appropriate for your ability/fitness, with plans for higher abilities containing more runs/week (and perhaps double-run days), a different mix of intensities, and longer durations

Where can you get training plans

Here are a few of the places you can get power-based plans:

- If you use the Stryd ecosystem, *[Stryd; Training Plans]* contains various plans for Running with Power.
- *[Final Surge; Training Plans]* has a good selection of power-based plans – search for "power".
- *[TrainingPeaks; Training Plans]* has a good selection of plans. The link searches for plans with "power" in the description.

There are many others (and I'm sure there will be many more) as Running with Power's popularity continues to grow.

Detraining

What's in this section?

Stopping or reducing your training will cause a partial or complete reversal of physical adaptations and will affect your performance ability.

The impact on your fitness is no different whether you train with power, heart rate or pace.

★ The difference is in the impact on your power metrics, which are quick to show performance gains but slow to show performance declines.

★ When you resume training, you may need to reset your modelled FTP/Auto-CP or switch to CP testing rather than modelled FTP or Auto-CP, rebuild your TSB/RSB data (60 days to be marginally useful, 80+ days to be valid), and use your Ramp Rate to avoid increasing your training too quickly, risking injury (or re-injury).

What happens if you stop or reduce your training?

It happens – you were working through a well-structured plan when you trip, fall, or twist an ankle and miss a few runs while recovering. Or maybe you miss runs due to sickness or needing to spend extra time at work or with family. Or perhaps you're deliberately reducing training (tapering) just before your goal event.

Stopping or reducing training (**detraining**) causes a partial or complete reversal of physical adaptations and will impact your performance ability. This happens whether it's due to injury, illness, or tapering – although tapering is a planned activity that deliberately balances the loss of training time against the time needed to recover from recent training fatigue.

Tapering is covered in the **Races & Events** chapter, while this section covers (unplanned) detraining due to injury or illness.

Stopping training for a week will have minimal impact, two weeks will have some impact, and stopping for 2-4 weeks will have a marked effect, although the timescales and effects may differ "in highly trained athletes with a training background of several years *[compared to]* recently trained but previously sedentary or moderately active individuals" *[Mujika and Padilla; Detraining - Part I (short-term)]*.

If you stop training for longer than 4 weeks, returning to the same fitness level may take longer than the period without training. However, "Reduced training strategies have been shown to delay the onset of cardiorespiratory, metabolic, muscular and hormonal detraining. Maintaining training intensity seems to be the key factor for the retention of training-induced physiological and performance adaptations" *[Mujika and Padilla; Detraining - Part II (long-term)]*.

What's different about detraining with power?

The impact on your fitness is no different whether you train with power, heart rate or pace.

What is different is the impact on your power metrics, which are quick to show performance gains but slow to show performance declines. This means that if you stop training for more than two weeks when you resume, you may need to use adjusted metrics, including:

- Resetting modelled FTP or Auto-CP or switching to CP testing. Modelled FTP and Auto-CP use your runs from the last 90 days to calculate CP/FTP, and if you're not training, your actual fitness will decline, while your modelled fitness will still be based on previous maximum efforts. When you return to training, you can reset your modelled FTP (e.g. using a different date range in WKO), ask for your Auto-CP to be reset (if using a Stryd), or use CP tests to establish a CP/FTP that better reflects your reduced fitness.

- Rebuilding your TSB/RSB. When starting to train with power, you need at least 60 days of TSS/RSS scores for TSB/RSB to be marginally useful and 80+ days of TSS/RSS scores for TSB/RSB to be valid. Stopping training has a similar effect, introducing a gap in your TSS/RSS scores, resulting in a more positive TSB/RSB. While this may appear to correctly reflect what's happened, the reality is that your TSB/RSB will contain a mix of TSS/RSS scores from two different training periods, won't reflect the full effect of your detraining and won't be reliable until you've consistently trained for another 60-80 days.

- Monitor your Ramp Rate. Your Ramp Rate is based on your Chronic Training Load (CTL)/42-day average. Stopping training will cause your Ramp Rate to become negative and eventually become zero, depending on how long you stop training. When you resume training, your Ramp Rate will become positive, and you should use your Ramp Rate to avoid increasing your training too quickly, risking injury (or re-injury).

Chapter 6

Power-Duration Curve

What's coming up?

The **Fundamentals** chapter presented the concept of effort domains and the phase transition (Threshold) between the heavy and severe domains. Below Threshold, you can maintain the intensity for 30 minutes or longer; above Threshold, you begin to fatigue much more quickly and need to slow down or stop, typically in 30 minutes or less.

But the domains were pretty broad – is there any way we could be more precise?

Of course, there is.

Here's a summary of what the chapter covers ...

Your Power-Duration (PD) Curve charts your theoretical power for every duration and enables you to identify your CP/FTP (within the Threshold phase transition)

When combined with your actual power over those same durations, your PD Curve enables you to *gain individualised insight into your relative strengths and weaknesses*.

Your PD Curve also enables the identification of your Time To Exhaustion (TTE) and your Reserve Work Capacity (RWC), which provide additional ways to *understand your individual capabilities* for shorter durations.

You can also determine your Riegel Exponent from your PD Curve. This allows you to *understand your individual capabilities* over longer durations.

This chapter starts with the relationship between Intensity and Duration, moves on to your PD Curve and how it's calculated from completed workouts, and then covers each metric derived from your PD Curve.

These metrics are used when planning event targets (covered in the **Races & Events** chapter)

The relationship between Intensity and Duration

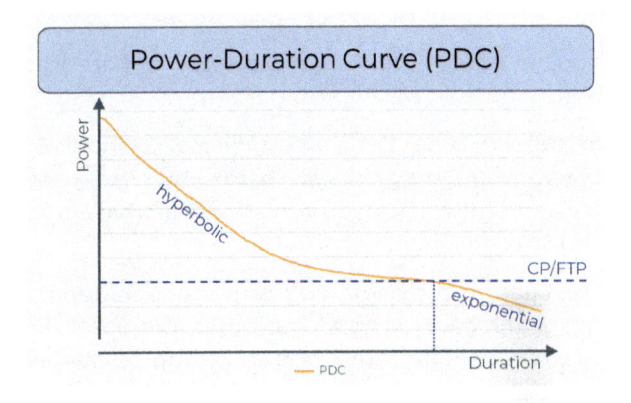

Power-Duration Curve (PDC)

Power (vertical axis), *hyperbolic*, *CP/FTP*, *exponential*, *Duration* (horizontal axis) — PDC

What's in this section?

Your Power-Duration Curve (PDC) shows your modelled power – what you could achieve – for different durations, with power on the vertical axis and duration on the horizontal axis.

You can maintain higher intensities for shorter durations or lower intensities for longer durations – there's an inverse relationship between power and duration.

The curve contains three distinct sections and can be used to derive several different metrics: CP/FTP, TTE, RWC, and the Riegel Exponent.

This section covers how the PDC was developed.

Higher Intensity means Shorter Duration

It's evident to anyone who's tried it: if you sprint, you can't sprint for a long time.

You have to choose. You can sprint for a short time or run more slowly for a longer time.

In other words, there's an inverse relationship between intensity (how hard you run) and duration (how long you run). If you increase one, you have to decrease the other.

The chart at the beginning of this section depicts this graphically (using a logarithmic duration scale to stretch shorter durations and compress longer durations). If you plot the power you're able to maintain against the durations for which you can maintain it, you arrive at a curve with three distinct sections:

- A hyperbolic curve at higher intensities (above CP/FTP).

- An exponential curve at lower intensities (below CP/FTP).

- An almost horizontal flat section (at or around CP/FTP), with your Time To Exhaustion at the crossover of the curve and your CP/FTP (the vertical dotted line).

Don't worry about the mathematical terms; they're not important.

As to how this curve was discovered, each of the three pieces is explored below.

Hyperbolic above CP/FTP

The hyperbolic curve at shorter durations comes from research into single muscle groups by [*Monod and Scherrer; The Work Capacity of a Synergic Muscular Group*], identifying Critical Power as "an exercise intensity that could be sustained for a very long time". Further research extended and validated the CP concept for whole-body exercise [*Hill; The Critical Power Concept*] while noting that "for a very long time" was usually 30 to 60 minutes of exercise at CP.

Monad and Scherrer also identified that the hyperbolic shape of the curve makes it "possible to define the maximum amount of work that can be performed in a given time as well as the conditions of work performed without fatigue". They called this maximum amount of work W' (pronounced W-prime). Other names used since include Anaerobic Work Capacity (AWC) and Functional Reserve Capacity (FRC).

In this book, I'll use the term Reserve Work Capacity (RWC), which Steve Palladino proposed and which nicely describes the concept.

The Reserve Work Capacity section in this chapter explores RWC.

Exponential below CP/FTP

The exponential curve at longer durations was identified by Peter Riegel *[Wikipedia; Peter Riegel]*, an American research engineer who, in 1977, developed a mathematical formula for predicting race times for runners given a specific performance at another distance. Riegel expanded on his thesis in 1981, stating that his formula concerned "activities in the 'endurance range', lasting between 3-5 and 230 minutes." *[Riegel; Athletic Records and Human Endurance]*.

Riegel's formula plots time vs. distance, but work by *[Van Dijk and Van Megen; The Power-Time Relationship]* concluded that a modified formula can describe the relationship between power and time.

The Riegel Exponent section in this chapter explores the modified formula, particularly the exponent (which defines the shape of the exponential curve).

The Power-Duration Curve

Andrew Coggan, PhD, completed the final piece of the puzzle, or more accurately, the work to bring the two curves together and place them in their relationship to CP/FTP. He developed a method for using maximum efforts from your workouts to chart a Mean-Max Power (MMP) curve that can be used as the basis for mathematically modelling your Power-Duration Curve.

Your Power-Duration Curve (PDC) "uses the relationship between time to exhaustion and work rate for both anaerobic and aerobic exercise, alongside your personal power data, to chart a complete curve of your power over all time periods" [*Allen, Coggan & McGregor; Power Duration Curve*], and can be used to gain insights into your relative strengths and weaknesses.

The Power-Duration Curve section in this chapter explores how your MMP is charted, how your PDC is derived from your MMP, and how the two provide those insights.

Power-Duration Curve (PDC)

PDC + Mean Max Power (MMP)

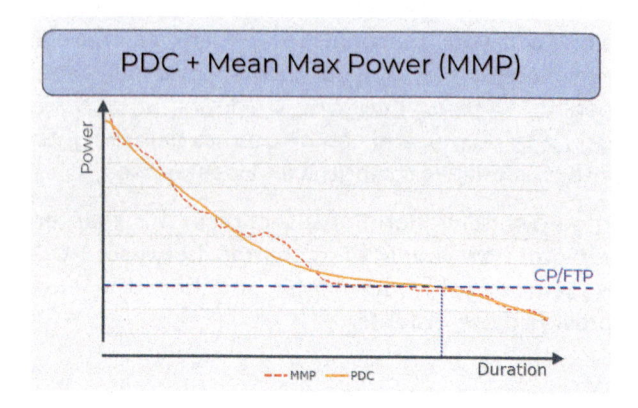

What's in this section?

Your Power-Duration Curve (PDC) shows your modelled power – what you could achieve – for different durations, with power on the vertical axis and duration on the horizontal axis.

★ Your PD Curve is personal, based on your workouts, and needs maximum efforts at a few different durations to be accurate.

Charting your MMP and PD curves together (see the chart above) can provide insights into your relative strengths and weaknesses.

Your PD Curve can be used to derive several different metrics: CP/FTP, TTE, RWC, and the Riegel Exponent.

Durations are often shown using a logarithmic scale, with shorter durations expanded and longer durations compressed.

What is it?

Your Power-Duration Curve (PDC) shows your modelled power – what you could achieve – for different durations, with power on the vertical axis and duration on the horizontal axis.

It combines the Critical Power hyperbolic curve with the Riegel exponential curve and identifies your CP/FTP using "the relationship between time to exhaustion and work rate for both anaerobic and aerobic exercise, alongside your personal power data, to chart a complete curve of your power overall time periods" *[Allen, Coggan & McGregor; Power Duration Curve]*.

Andrew Coggan, PhD, developed the PDC and a method for using maximum workout efforts to chart a Mean-Max Power Curve (MMP) that can be used as the basis for modelling your PDC.

Why is it needed?

So that you can gain insight into your relative strengths and weaknesses and track training progress.

The PDC is *your* curve, unique to you and based on the Power-Duration values you can generate, rather than being based on population averages of hundreds of runners with no clue how fit they were, which events they were training for, etc.

Charting your MMP and PDC together can provide insights into your relative strengths and weaknesses for your current fitness level.

You can also track training progress by comparing your current PDC to earlier PDCs.

Finally, your PDC is the basis for several other metrics.

How to measure or calculate it?

As you run, your watch (or mobile phone) will record your second-by-second power. That information can be used to identify your maximum power for different durations and to chart a Mean-Max Power (MMP) curve – the red dotted line in the chart at the beginning of this section.

Your PDC is a line that smooths out your MMP curve – either a line touching the MMP maximums or a line of best fit running between MMP maximums and minimums – the orange solid line in the chart at the beginning of this section.

Your MMP Curve shows what you *have* achieved; your PDC models what you *could* achieve.

Importantly, you don't need to calculate your PDC yourself – many apps will do the calculation for you. All you need to do is feed in your completed workouts (including some maximum efforts).

If you'd like to know how those apps calculate your MMP and PDC, see "How is your PDC calculated?" below.

How to use it?

Several metrics can be derived from your PD Curve:

- Reserve Work Capacity (RWC) – the area of a rectangle under your PDC and above CP/FTP.
- Critical Power or Functional Threshold Power (CP/FTP) – the middle, flatter part of the PDC.
- Time To Exhaustion (TTE) – the point where your CP/FTP crosses your PDC.
- Riegel Exponent – the exponent driving the shape of your PDC at intensities below CP/FTP.

CP/FTP is covered in the **Fundamentals** chapter; the other metrics are covered in this chapter.

In addition, by calculating your PDC from your MMP, you don't have to run maximum efforts at every duration – it's enough to run maximum efforts at 3-4 different durations, as long as those durations are well-chosen (for example, 20-30 seconds, 2-3 minutes, 10-12 minutes, 20-25 minutes).

Even better, you can complete one maximum effort every few weeks, using the individual results to keep your PDC updated and to track training progress.

As you improve, you'll be capable of holding a higher power at each duration, the same power for a longer duration, or both. Your PDC will change as you change, reflecting your current ability at each point in your training – if you're improving, it will move "up and to the right". More often, based on the mix of intensities in your training and when you run your maximum efforts, different parts of the curve will move at different times.

How is your PD Curve calculated?

As you run, your watch records second-by-second power readings from your power meter.

Imagine taking those power readings, picking a duration (perhaps 3 minutes) and calculating the average or mean power for the first 3 minutes of your workout. Then imagine calculating the mean power for the 3 minutes that started one second later, then the mean power for the 3 minutes that started another second later and so on until you've calculated the mean power for the last three minutes of your workout. The result would be several different 3-minute mean power numbers, each starting one second later than the previous. The maximum of these numbers would represent your 3-minute Mean-Maximum Power for the workout.

Now imagine doing that for all your workouts over the last 90 days – you'd end up with the three-minute Mean-Maximum Power for every workout longer than 3 minutes. The maximum of those per-workout numbers would represent your 90-day 3-minute Mean-Maximum Power.

Of course, to be meaningful, your 3-minute Mean-Maximum Power should be based on a real 3-

minute maximum rather than on a maximum you set while running and chatting with friends. To state that another way, your 3-minute Mean-Maximum Power should be based on a maximum effort – a run when you were actively working to achieve your 3-minute best.

Now imagine calculating Mean-Maximum Power values for 2 minutes, 1 minute, 30 seconds, etc., and in the other direction, doing it for 4 minutes, 5 minutes, 10 minutes (and so on).

If you charted the results for all those different durations, with power on the vertical axis and duration on the horizontal, then joined up each value, you'd be charting your Mean-Maximum Power Curve (**MMP**) – the red dotted line in the chart at the beginning of this section.

It wouldn't be a smooth curve. Instead, you'd probably find flat sections with the same Mean-Maximum Power value over a range of durations and "jumps" or "steps", where your Mean-Maximum Power value changed suddenly from one duration to the next. The shape of the line would depend on the workouts, testing and racing you'd completed over the last 90 days and where (within your completed runs) the Mean-Maximum Power values were found.

Finally, imagine using some maths to smooth out the MMP (this kind of smoothing is called regression). The smoothed curve is your Power-Duration Curve (**PDC**) – the orange solid line in the chart at the beginning of this section.

You could choose to draw your smoothed curve representing the "best fit" between your MMP's highs and lows – sometimes the curve would be below the MMP line, sometimes above, but on balance, it would represent the curve that stayed closest to all of the MMP highs and lows.

Or you could draw a smoothed curve touching all of your MMP's highs – a line of "theoretical maximums" across the top of your MMP. Where it touched an MMP point, it would represent the maximum you'd achieved; between the high points, it would represent a maximum you may be able to achieve.

Maximum effort runs

★ If your PDC is a line based on your MMP, and your MMP shows the maximum power values you achieved for each duration, then for your PDC to accurately model what you could achieve, you need to include some **maximum efforts** in your training. An accurate PDC usually needs a minimum of 4 maximum efforts, each with durations of different orders of magnitude (for example, 20-30 seconds, 2-3 minutes, 10-12 minutes, 20-25 minutes).

Logarithmic durations

Drawing your PDC with a linear horizontal axis gives a hyperbolic curve, with nothing much appearing to happen at longer durations and without the three distinct sections.

For this reason, PDCs are drawn using a logarithmic scale. This stretches the shorter durations and compresses the longer durations, allowing you to see the two distinct (and different) curves.

Reserve Work Capacity (RWC)

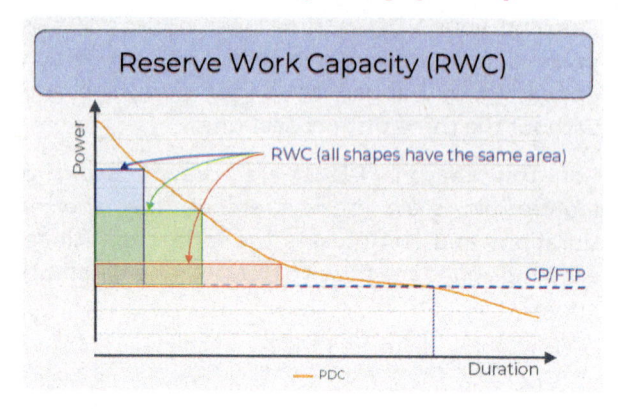

What's in this section?

Reserve Work Capacity (RWC) is the Work you can do above CP/FTP [*Palladino; Reserve Work Capacity*] where Work = Power * Duration.

Run above CP/FTP, and you deplete your RWC; run below, and your RWC recovers. If you use up your RWC, you will have no choice but to run below CP/FTP.

★ RWC is important for events where your effort exceeds CP/FTP (either throughout, e.g. 1500m or 5k, or with surges above CP/FTP). It can be used to plan the target power for the event and to estimate your finish time.

What is it?

Reserve Work Capacity (**RWC**) "is the amount of Work that can be done above CP/FTP" *[Palladino; Reserve Work Capacity]*.

Think of your RWC as a barrel of water (with the water representing energy).

When you run at a power above CP/FTP, you drain the barrel. The speed with which it drains depends on how far in excess of CP/FTP you are running.

When you run at a power below CP/FTP, internal metabolic processes refill the barrel. The speed with which it refills depends on how far below CP/FTP you are running, with refilling slowing the closer you get to full recovery.

If you empty the barrel, you have no choice but to slow down – the energy you need to run above CP/FTP is fully depleted.

Why is it needed?

So that you can plan your target power and estimate your finish time for shorter events.

RWC is important for events where your effort exceeds CP/FTP (either throughout, e.g., 1500m or 5k, or with surges above CP/FTP).

How to measure or calculate it?

RWC is calculated for any Power-Duration point above CP/FTP as (Power – CP/FTP) * Duration

with the result expressed in kilojoules (kJ).

★ Your RWC is the area of a rectangle under your PDC and above CP/FTP, with one corner touching your PDC.

The curve above CP/FTP is hyperbolic, meaning that the area of any rectangle sitting under PDC and above CP/FTP will be the same, regardless of which Power-Duration point is chosen.

Power-duration models typically report both CP/FTP and RWC estimates. The Stryd platform does not report RWC, even though its power-duration model could produce an RWC estimate.

How to use it?

The **Races & Events** chapter describes how your RWC can be used to estimate a finish time for a shorter event (where you'll be running at an effort above CP/FTP).

Further information

RWC cannot be calculated using Power-Duration pairs below CP/FTP. RWC is an "above CP/FTP" concept.

RWC can differ for each runner – even two runners with the same CP/FTP.

For example, suppose two runners have the same CP/FTP, but one has a higher RWC than the other. If both ran a 3-minute maximum effort time trial, the runner with the higher RWC would produce a higher average power for that 3-minute time trial.

RWC is equivalent to W-Prime (W´), Anaerobic Work Capacity (AWC) and Functional Reserve Capacity (FRC) [*Allen, Coggan & McGregor; Functional Reserve Capacity*].

Riegel Exponent

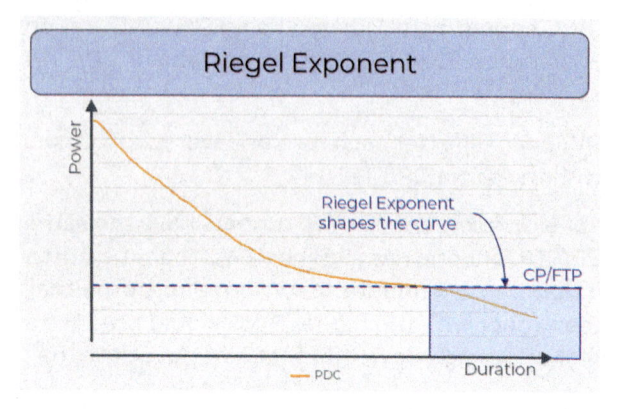

Figure: Riegel Exponent — Power vs Duration curve (PDC) showing Riegel Exponent shapes the curve, with CP/FTP threshold indicated.

What's in this section?

The Riegel formula was initially developed to predict race times based on performances at other distances. It models the relationship between speed and distance.

A modified power-based formula models the relationship between power and duration, primarily for endurance (rather than sprint) durations.

The formula produces an exponential curve, with the shape of the curve dependent on the exponent value. The exponent can be used as a measure of fatigue resistance at longer durations.

★ Your Riegel Exponent is important for events where your effort is below CP/FTP – events lasting longer than 30 minutes or so – and can be used to estimate your finish time for that longer event.

What is it?

The Riegel Formula models the exponential relationship between speed and distance when running at endurance effort levels *[Riegel; Athletic Records and Human Endurance]* and enables finish-time predictions for an event based on performances at other distances.

A modified formula models the relationship between power and duration *[Van Dijk and Van Megen; The Power-Time Relationship]* and enables finish-time predictions based on a runner's CP/FTP and Running Effectiveness.

Your **Riegel Exponent** determines the shape of the exponential curve, with exponents closer to zero producing flatter curves and exponents further from zero producing steeper curves – a flatter curve (exponent closer to zero) indicates better fatigue resistance.

Why is it needed?

So that you can plan your target power and estimate your finish time for longer events.

Your Riegel Exponent is important for events where your effort is below CP/FTP – events lasting longer than 30 minutes or so.

How to measure or calculate it?

The original Riegel formula was:

$V_2 / V_1 = (D_2 / D_1) \wedge E$

where V is speed (metres/second), D is distance (metres), and E is an exponent (which Riegel found to be 1.06 for elite athletes). By rearranging the formula and using age-adjusted values for the exponent, online race prediction websites can provide predicted race times for a marathon (for example) based on your age and a 10k finish time.

A similar formula for use with power *[Van Dijk and Van Megen; The Power-Time Relationship]* predicts the power a runner can hold for a given duration, given another power-duration pair.

The formula is:

$P_2 = P_1 * (T_2 / T_1) \wedge E$

where P is power (Watts), T is time (Seconds), and E is an exponent (which Van Dijk and Van Megen found to be -0.07 for elite athletes).

The exponent can be used as a measure of your fatigue resistance at longer durations.

The formula works best when you run at effort levels at or below CP/FTP, with minimal impact from RWC.

★ To calculate *your* Riegel Exponent, choose any two points on your PDC that are below CP/FTP (for example, 95% and 90% of CP/FTP, then use the following formula:

E = Log(T2 / T1) of P2 / P1

where P is power (Watts), T is time (seconds), E is the exponent, and the Logarithm base is T2 / T1

How to use it?

Your Riegel Exponent is a valuable indicator of improving (or declining) fatigue resistance over longer durations, even if your CP/FTP remains unchanged.

The **Races & Events** chapter describes how your Riegel Exponent can be used to estimate a finish time for a longer event (where you'll be running at an effort below CP/FTP).

Which exponent should I use?

Riegel charted his results using an exponent of 1.06 (time vs distance) and converting to power vs time; the equivalent value is -0.07. *[Van Dijk and Van Megen; The Power-Time Relationship]* confirm that this value is "valid for the world records of both men and women".

Like CP/FTP and RWC, Riegel exponents vary across runners because fatigue resistance (aka endurance) varies across runners.

You can calculate *your* exponent using the formula above. Or you can use Palladino's Riegel tables in the SuperPower Calculator for Sheets *[SPC for Sheets]*, which provides values based on prior race results (with the exponent ranging from -0.03 through -0.12).

Time To Exhaustion (TTE)

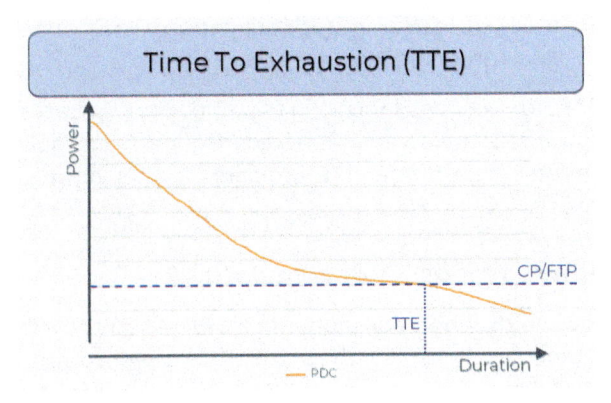

Figure: Time To Exhaustion (TTE) — Power Duration Curve (PDC) showing TTE as the duration at which power drops below CP/FTP.

What's in this section?

Time To Exhaustion (TTE) is defined as the duration for which you can maintain CP/FTP, although TTE can be applied to any intensity, e.g. TTE at 110% of CP/FTP or TTE at VO2max power.

TTE values are typically 50 minutes +/- 20 minutes.

TTE is a measure of fatigue resistance for shorter durations.

What is it?

Time To Exhaustion (**TTE**) is "the maximum duration for which a power equal to model-derived FTP can be maintained" *[Allen, Coggan & McGregor; Time To Exhaustion]*

Why is it needed?

So that you can monitor your fatigue resistance (aka endurance) for shorter events.

TTE measures fatigue resistance for shorter durations; a lower TTE indicates lower fatigue resistance; a higher TTE indicates higher fatigue resistance.

How to measure or calculate it?

It's the duration component of CP/FTP on the PD Curve and occurs when the PD curve crosses CP/FTP.

How to use it?

TTE is a useful indicator of improving (or declining) fatigue resistance over shorter durations, even if your CP/FTP remains unchanged.

Further information

It's different for each runner – even for two runners with the same CP/FTP who can achieve the same maximal power.

CP/FTP TTE values are typically 50 minutes +/- 20 minutes, with recreational racers typically clustering towards the lower half and elite runners typically clustering towards the upper half.

It is possible to calculate TTE for power values other than CP/FTP, e.g. TTE at VO2max power or TTE at 110% CP/FTP.

Chapter 7

Races & Events

What's coming up?

Power measures your effort. Combined with duration, it indicates how long you can run at each effort level.

But most races are run over distance (not duration). Given an event distance, how can you estimate your finish time?

And if Running with Power "gives you the greatest chance of achieving *your* best performance," how do you use power to identify your optimum target, arrive at the start with fresh legs, and avoid going with the crowd (and the adrenaline) in the early stages of an event?

Here's a summary of what the chapter covers ...

Running Effectiveness, which measures how effectively you convert power to speed (your speed:power ratio), can be used to estimate the distance you'd cover for any Power-Duration combination. Coupled with your CP/FTP and your Riegel Exponent or your Reserve Work Capacity (depending on the event distance), you can use Running Effectiveness to *plan your event target* and *estimate your expected finish time.*

As you approach your event, the training metrics covered in the **Training** chapter can be used to *plan your taper* so that you maximise your training while arriving at the start with fresh legs, ready to run your best.

At the event, power enables you to target a consistent effort based on your current fitness. That target isn't affected by hills or wind as it's based on the effort you can maintain – of course, hills and wind have an impact, but the effect is on your finish time, not on *maintaining your power target.*

Running Effectiveness (RE)

What's in this section?

RE measures how effectively you convert power into speed (your speed:power ratio).

★ RE can be used to track improvements over time, estimate an event finish time, monitor the impact of working on your form, and compare runners or running shoes.

★ RE is impacted by intensity, grade and wind (to name a few).

What is it?

Your Running Effectiveness (**RE**) measures how effectively you convert power into speed (your speed:power ratio).

Running Effectiveness was proposed by Andrew Coggan, PhD [*Coggan; WKO4: New Metrics for Running With Power*].

Why is it needed?

So that you can plan your target power and estimate your finish time for all event distances – RE relates Power-Duration to Distance.

RE is a field-based measure conceptually similar to but distinctly different from Running Economy (oxygen consumption at various speeds) and Running Efficiency (external mechanical power vs. metabolic power production), which both require lab-based testing.

How to measure or calculate it?

It is calculated as the ratio of speed to power: RE = speed (m/s) / power (W/kg)

where speed is in metres per second, and power is in Watts per kilogram.

How to use it?

RE can be used:

- to evaluate a workout (or part of a workout) or to compare two different workouts or parts of workouts. RE can gauge fatigue (higher RE at the start of a workout, lower at the end) and track improvements in fatigue resistance.

- to estimate time from planned power and distance or the power needed to finish a race in a goal time. RE links power and speed; speed is based on distance and time. The RE calculation can be rearranged to use three values to calculate the fourth, e.g., time from power, distance, and RE, power from distance, time, and RE, or pace/speed from RE and power.

- to assess the impact of working on your form. If you're working on your form (perhaps using drills or plyometrics), you can use RE to gauge whether you're becoming more effective at converting power to speed (or less effective!)

- to compare runners. Different runner's RE values can be used to gauge who might have greater potential for higher speed as long as the RE values are normalised to a runner-specific intensity (e.g. CP/FTP) over a flat course with minimal wind.

- to compare shoes. It's possible to measure RE for different shoes to see which produces a higher RE, again taking care to account for differences in intensity, grade, and wind.

Further information

From *[Coggan; WKO4: New Metrics for Running With Power]*, "Running Effectiveness may be lower in novice or fatigued runners since they do not travel as fast for a given power output or must generate more power to achieve the same speed."

Running Effectiveness is impacted by:

- power meter. Because there is no agreed standard for running power meters, the power reported by each meter may include (or exclude) different elements – for example, later generations of the Stryd footpod incorporate Air Power. In contrast, Garmin's algorithm does not have air power but may include estimated energy from elastic return. In other words, RE is hardware-specific.

- intensity. Your RE when jogging may differ from your RE when running or when sprinting. Differences in your running form affect how effectively you convert power at those different speeds. RE typically increases at higher intensities.

- grade. When running uphill, your power will be higher for the same speed (or will remain the same, but your speed will be lower) – and your RE (speed/power) will be lower. The reverse is true when running downhill.
- wind. Similarly, when running into a headwind, your power will be higher for the same speed (or will remain the same, but your speed will be lower), which means that your RE (speed/power) will be lower. The reverse is true when running with a tailwind.

☺ More information about Running Effectiveness can be found in *[Palladino; Understanding 'Running Effectiveness' and its uses]*.

Setting event targets

What's in this section?

Power is used with Duration (Power-Duration), not Distance. But most events are run over known distances (5k, 10k etc.) To plan distance-based event targets, we need some way to relate Power-Duration to Distance.

The percentage of CP/FTP can give a first-pass estimate of race power and estimated finish time, but that estimate is not individualised and may not be accurate across a broad population of runners.

The Stryd race power planner can provide a more accurate target race power than the percentage of CP/FTP, but it's not clear whether it differentiates between shorter events and longer events and whether it uses your RWC for shorter events, without which the planner will become less accurate the shorter the event.

Super-Power Calculator for Sheets can identify best-case, worst-case, and most likely scenarios with visibility of all inputs and outputs. It has calculators for both shorter and longer events.

★ All methods depend on having an accurate and recent CP/FTP and information about your Running Effectiveness; depending on the chosen model, you may also need to know your RWC or Riegel Exponent.

What does an event target depend on?

You're planning to run a 10k. You know the distance (it's 10k). You might have a feel for your finish time – let's imagine it's somewhere around an hour. From your Power-Duration Curve (PDC), you can determine the power you could maintain for an hour. And that can be your target.

But that target is based on your estimate of your finish time ... that it might take an hour.

What if you could run it in less time? Then, from your PDC, you'd be able to (and need to) run it at a higher power. Is that your target? What if it might take longer instead? That would be a lower power target!

We need some way to relate the distance to duration so that you can determine your target power or some way to relate the distance to power so that you can estimate your finish time.

Percentage of CP/FTP

One way to convert the distance to a power value is to use standardised estimates based on population averages – for example, "most runners run a 10k at around 100-104% of their CP/FTP" or "most runners run a marathon at around 91-94% of their CP/FTP".

[Palladino; Race power as a percentage of FTP/CP] explores this in detail and provides several data tables showing CP/FTP ranges for various race distances and runner groups.

The article also points out, however, that the percentage depends on having a valid and recent CP/FTP and that there will be variation across individuals depending on the following:

- their ability to convert power to speed – a higher Running Effectiveness (RE) will translate into a shorter duration (and therefore a higher percentage of CP/FTP)
- whether the event is shorter than the runner's Time To Exhaustion (TTE) at CP/FTP – in this case, the runner's Reserve Work Capacity (RWC) will impact the finish time, with a higher RWC translating into a shorter duration
- whether the event is longer than the runner's Time To Exhaustion (TTE) at CP/FTP – in this case, the runner's Riegel Exponent (their fatigue resistance) will impact the finish time, with a less negative exponent translating into a shorter duration
- the environmental conditions (heat, humidity, altitude, wind) compared to those that were in place when the runner's CP/FTP was calculated – higher temperatures, higher humidities, higher altitudes and higher wind speeds will all translate into longer durations

TTE, RWC and your Riegel exponent are covered in the **Power-Duration Curve** chapter; Running Effectiveness is covered earlier in this chapter.

★ Percentage of CP/FTP may be able to give a first-pass estimate of race power and estimated finish time, but that estimate may not be accurate once all of the above are considered.

You need a different model for a more individualised target power and estimated finish time.

The Stryd race power planner

If you use the Stryd footpod, the Stryd ecosystem includes the web-based *[Stryd; Race Calculator (PowerCenter)]* and the *[Stryd; Race Calculator (mobile)]*.

The Race Calculator uses your workouts from the last 90 days, your Auto-CP and (optionally) information about the event course and the expected environmental conditions. It produces a best-case target power and an estimate of your finish time.

Your workout data must meet some requirements *[Stryd; Race Calculator requirements]* to get an accurate target power.

These are:

- A valid course, uploaded via PowerCenter – to consider hills and their impact on your Running Effectiveness.

- An accurate CP – representing your current metabolic fitness.

- At least one workout containing intensities around your CP – to determine your Running Effectiveness at/around your CP.

- At least one workout containing intensities close to your estimated event intensity – to determine your Running Effectiveness at/around your estimated intensity.

- An accurate model curve between 10 and 20 minutes – to model your fatigue resistance, most likely using the Riegel model.

★ The Stryd race power planner can provide a more accurate target race power than the percentage of CP/FTP, but it's not clear whether it differentiates between shorter events (taking less than 30 minutes or so, e.g. 1500m, 5k) and longer events and crucially, whether it uses your RWC for shorter events, without which the planner will become less accurate the shorter the event.

In addition, the Stryd race power planner does not support planning events longer than 50km.

You need a different model if you want to plan a shorter or a very long event or if you want to have complete control over the choice of calculation and the calculation inputs.

Race power scenarios using SuperPower Calculator

If you don't use the Stryd ecosystem, or you'd like complete control over the choice of model, its inputs, and how those impact the event power target, you can use SuperPower Calculator for Sheets (SPCS) *[SPC for Sheets]*.

SPCs provides two different Race Power models:

- For shorter events (less than your TTE at CP/FTP), "Generate Race Power Scenarios using FTP/CP, RWC (W') and Running Effectiveness" uses your CP/FTP, your RWC and a few different Running Effectiveness numbers to calculate race power scenarios – each scenario provides a race power target, the equivalent percentage of your CP/FTP and an estimate of your finish time. [*Palladino; Race Planning using RWC and RE*] is a YouTube video showing how to use SPCs for shorter events.

- For longer events (more than your TTE at CP/FTP), "Generate Race Power Scenarios using pairs of Riegel Exponents and Running Effectiveness" calculates race power scenarios using your CP/FTP, a few different Riegel Exponents and a few different Running Effectiveness numbers. Each scenario provides a race power target, the equivalent percentage of your CP/FTP, and an estimate of your finish time. [*Palladino; Race Planning using Riegel Exponents and RE*] is a YouTube video showing using SPCs for longer events.

★ You can use SPCs to identify best-case, worst-case, and most likely scenarios with visibility of all inputs and outputs.

What's different about power-based event targets?

As you will have gathered, race power planning differs from planning an event using pace or heart rate. The following are the key differences:

- Your target depends heavily on your CP/FTP. No surprise here. Race power planning is based on *your* metabolic fitness.

- The model used to calculate your target may differ depending on whether it's a shorter or a longer event. This matches the different sections of your PDC – the hyperbolic section using RWC for shorter durations and the exponential section using your Riegel Exponent for longer durations.

- Your target depends on your expected finish time (Power-Duration), which depends on how effectively you convert power to speed – your Running Effectiveness.

This may seem complicated – it is. Your body is complex, and the calculators described above try to consider many factors to estimate target power and finish time.

★ They are estimates. But they're estimates based on *your* completed workouts, *your* metabolic fitness, and *your* ability to convert power to speed.

★ They're based on you, not on population averages.

★ And they're based on actual data, not on guesswork or a desire for a specific goal time (which may or may not be achievable).

This, for me, is one of the most significant benefits of Running with Power.

Tapering

What's in this section?

Tapering aims to achieve a controlled reduction in your training so that your body has time to recover from the fatigue, enabling you to arrive at the start line for your event "on fresh legs".

An exponential taper that maintains exposure to intensity while reducing volume exponentially has been demonstrated to be "best".

You can use your Stress Balance (TSB or RSB) and Ramp Rate to plan your taper.

The aim of tapering

The **Training** chapter describes what happens when you train. Each workout causes stress, providing a stimulus for your body to adapt. The stress produces longer-term and shorter-term responses.

Tapering aims to achieve a controlled reduction in your training so that your body has time to recover from the fatigue, enabling you to arrive at the start line for your event "on fresh legs".

As usual, it's a balance. Start the taper too soon, and you'll miss out on training; too late, you'll arrive with tired or heavy legs.

How to plan your taper

Running with Power uses your workout data to plan your taper, focusing on two metrics that, in combination, can be used to plan a partial taper (for a B race) or a full taper (for your A race). The two metrics are:

- Your Training Stress Balance or Running Stress Balance (depending on which set of metrics you're using), showing the balance between shorter-term fatigue and longer-term adaptation, with a positive Stress Balance indicating your training may be too easy, a slightly negative Stress Balance indicating "productive" training and a very negative Stress Balance indicating you may be at risk of over-training or injury. As you approach your goal event, you can plan your workouts so that your Stress Balance becomes more positive, ready for the event.

- Your Ramp Rate, measuring the change in your Chronic Training Load (CTL) or your 42-day weighted average (depending on which metrics you're using). Increases in CTL/42-day average produce a positive Ramp Rate; decreases produce a negative Ramp Rate. As you approach your goal event, you can plan your workouts so that your Ramp Rate becomes more negative, ready for the event.

For both metrics, you should use forecast numbers based on the stress scores for your planned workouts and look ahead to the numbers that will be in place on the event day.

The obvious question is, what numbers should you use as taper targets for your training balance and ramp rate?

☺ This depends on the event duration (shorter events generally need a shorter taper) and how the event factors into your longer-term plans.

★ If it's your 'A' race (the event you've been training for), you might aim for a positive training balance *and* a negative ramp rate. This will (and should) mean you "give up" some training leading up to the event.

★ If it's a 'B' race (an event you may be using to test fitness or race-day strategy), you might aim for a training balance somewhere around zero but maintain a positive rather than a negative ramp rate. This would involve scaling back your training but not giving up too much.

Is there anything else I should consider?

There are lots of things! But most of them are no different when Running with Power than when running using pace or heart rate. Here are a few from *[Fellrnr; Practical Tapering]*:

- Reducing intensity during your taper may *reduce* your performance, rather than improving it – you should maintain exposure to higher intensity.

- Reduce your training volume (the time you spend training) exponentially during the taper period, with larger reductions at the start and smaller reductions towards the end, aiming for an overall 20-40% reduction.

- There is a high level of individual variability, depending on the goal event, the training plan, and the runner's physiology. Some experimentation may be needed to find your optimum taper period and training volume reduction.

- Be prepared to feel sluggish and for new aches and pains to make themselves known. It's all part of adjusting to less exercise.

In addition:

- Fellrnr advises that for longer events (half-marathon or above), a 2-week taper is ideal, while 3 weeks or longer may *reduce* your performance rather than improving it; for shorter events, a 1-week taper may be enough. When Running with Power, you can use Stress Balance and Ramp Rate to achieve a taper that is individual to you and matches whether it's your 'A' race or a 'B' event.

- During the taper, reduce your cross-training, cutting out lower-body strength training from the start of your taper and all strength training in the final week before your event. Continue with stretching and mobility work throughout.

- You may also want to consider changes to nutrition, although there's little research on this. And be prepared for a small weight gain – this is an expected side effect of reducing your training volume and building up your energy stores.

The event

What's in this section?

For your watch display, less is more. This will help reduce confusion or overthinking when you're fatigued in the later stages of the event.

Resist the temptation to include elapsed time, time of day, pace, or heart rate on your watch, as this may distract you from maintaining a power target.

Use your pre-event warm-up to "wake up" your three energy-producing systems (aerobic, anaerobic/lactic and alactic/phosphagen)

Monitor your power more frequently during the first stages of an event to avoid going out too fast.

Aim to run just under your target for 50-75% of the event, then (if you're feeling good) slowly increase your power during the final stages to achieve a positive power split.

Setting up your watch

What you see on your watch is vitally important when running an event. This is especially true in the later stages of an event, when you may be tired and more easily confused.

Deciding what to show on your watch is a personal thing. Some prefer to see more, others less. I'm in the "less is more" camp, and this approach works well with a power target.

The **Workouts** chapter has a section on your watch display. At the end of that section, it describes a progression many runners seem to go through; eventually, landing on less is more.

☺ I would recommend setting up your watch to:

- show lap power and 3-second or 10-second power

- if possible, also show last-lap power (so that you aren't forced to look at your watch every auto-lap

- auto-lap every mile or kilometre (depending on your preference and the race distance)

Including other metrics on your watch display

☺ Why not show elapsed time (since you started your event) or time of day? Because this will distract you from maintaining a power target, shifting your focus onto hitting a goal time, regardless of whether or not you'll be able to achieve that time. Don't do it.

☺ Why not show heart rate as well as power? Because this will distract you from maintaining a power target, shifting your focus onto maintaining a lower heart rate, regardless of whether or not the event conditions or your physical condition (stress, anxiety, lack of sleep) are impacting your heart rate. Don't do it.

☺ Why not show pace as well as power? Because this will distract you from maintaining a power target, shifting your focus onto maintaining a specific pace, regardless of whether or not you'll be able to maintain that pace. Don't do it.

And, of course, make sure your watch and power meter are fully charged!

Warming up

Your body isn't a machine – you can't just "turn it on" and expect to be able to run at your target power. Switching from *not running* to *running smoothly* requires a warm-up. Depending on your event distance, you may even need to prime two or more energy-producing systems in your body.

Your warm-up should include dynamic stretching and 5-10 minutes of jogging. So far, nothing different than warming up when using pace or heart rate rather than power.

★ After the dynamic stretching and jogging, you should run some short intervals at varying intensities – perhaps at 98-100% CP/FTP (to wake up your aerobic system), at 102-105% CP/FTP (to wake up your anaerobic/lactic system), finishing with some accelerations (to wake up your alactic/phosphagen system). And remember to include a couple of minutes between each interval to recover.

You should complete your warm-up well before having to line up at the start (or at the start gates) – your various power production systems will remain "triggered" for an hour or so.

And if you find yourself standing around waiting for a staggered start, you can always bounce on the spot to keep your body warm and your legs loose.

Going out too fast (or too slow)

At the start of an event, with fresh legs and hundreds of other runners around (who all seem to be running faster than you), it can be easy to get carried along with the crowd. Before you know it, you've unintentionally set new personal bests for the first part of a much longer event. As a result, the second half of the event can be harsh on tired legs.

With a power target, you can avoid going out too fast. If you keep to your target, a target that you know you can maintain for the entire event, you can remain confident that you're running at the right intensity for your current metabolic fitness and that you don't need to keep up with the rest of the runners.

Occasionally, you may experience the opposite problem – there are so many runners that it's congested, and you can't run at your target power. It can be tempting to try to "make up" for the slower start by running above your target. Don't do it.

Going out slower, at a power below your target, may even be a good thing …

Managing your power

Your race target is an estimate. It's a very good estimate based on your CP/FTP and actual workout data, but it's an estimate. And while it might include many different factors, there are still more that it can't consider, such as stress, lack of sleep, fatigue, adrenaline, stimulants, humidity, heat, cold, and hydration.

☺ You should probably treat your target power as a "best estimate" and plan your event accordingly.

How?

You may have heard about "negative splits", especially if you've watched elite runners in marathon and half-marathon events. A negative split occurs when the runner completes the second half of the event faster than the first half.

☺ Running with Power has a similar concept – the "positive power split". A positive power split is when you run the second half of an event at a higher power than the first half. To achieve this, you could choose to run 1-2% below your "best estimate" power target for the first 50-75% of the event; then, if you're still feeling good (and have some energy in reserve), you could run 1-2% above your power target, finishing the event strong.

☺ Whether you use a positive power split is entirely your choice. What you should not do is decide to run above your "best effort" power right from the start. Don't do it. Otherwise, you'll most likely struggle during the later parts of the event, having given too much early on.

★ Power enables you to determine the race-day target that will produce *the best result based on your fitness*. It will also enable you to run the race at an effort level *you can maintain throughout*.

What's different about running events with power?

★ When you run events, you run to a power target – you won't (you shouldn't) run to a goal time. Power targets are based on your current metabolic fitness and are much better aligned with what you can achieve than a goal time that may be based on wishful thinking. This is probably the most significant difference, and if you've been used to using goal times, running an event without a time to aim for can be very disconcerting.

Running to power targets *also* means you won't be able to run with pacers. Pacers aim to finish in a specific time – your finish time will depend on your fitness (from your training), your power target, your Running Effectiveness and your race-day execution.

Your target is your target. You don't need to adjust your power if you encounter hills or wind – you just need to stay on target.

★ What's also different is the confidence that Running with Power can give you. Your targets are based on *your* fitness, which is based on *your* completed workouts, *your* ability to convert power to speed, and *your* Power-Duration Curve. Everything is individualised.

This is quite different than looking up a potential goal time using a table compiled using data from thousands of runners (many of which will be nothing like you).

Chapter 8

Environments

What's coming up?

I love running a gently undulating route on a cool, crisp morning with a gentle breeze. These are perfect running conditions.

Unfortunately, not every run will take place in perfect conditions.

Here's a summary of what the chapter covers ...

This chapter examines the impacts of different environmental conditions and covers adjustments that can be made to account for these differences – for example:

- Running on a treadmill – an environment with much less wind (even gym fans aren't *really* windy) and potentially much higher temperature and humidity than usual, and with no access to GPS to determine your speed.

- Running in locations close to the equator in the local summertime – an environment which may lead to extended periods with very high temperature/humidity.

- Running in the mountains – an environment that may be cooler than usual but where altitude (above sea level) may have a measurable effect.
- Running a trail or ultra event – an environment with lots of elevation changes, some being quite steep, forcing hiking rather than running, and often over technical routes and carrying extra weight (water, emergency supplies, etc.)

These environments differ from those you may be used to because of differences in temperature, humidity, altitude, wind, weight, or access to GPS.

So what? These changes have always been an issue for runners!

When Running with Power, the impact of some of these can be quantified and included (at least a little).

Heat, Humidity and Altitude

What's in this section?

If you run in a hot, humid place at your usual effort level, you'll get hot quicker, sweat more, not be able to cool down as quickly and may become dehydrated. These will all limit your performance compared to your typical environment.

If you run at a higher altitude than usual, you'll get less oxygen to your muscles, limiting your performance compared to your typical environment.

When running in hotter, more humid, or higher altitude conditions, your CP/FTP will be overstated, which will overstate your targets.

When running in cooler, less humid, or lower altitude conditions, your CP/FTP will be understated, which will understate your targets.

You can calculate adjustment percentages using [*SPC for Sheets*]. At the end of this section, a link to a YouTube video explains how to do this.

What happens when you run in heat or humidity?

When you run, energy-producing reactions in your body generate heat, which raises your body temperature. This reduces the efficiency of the energy-producing reactions, which work best within a certain range of temperatures. Your body diverts blood to your skin, where it can be cooled through sweating and evaporation. The cooled blood lowers your body temperature when it returns to your core.

In hotter environments, you start with a hotter body temperature, which already impacts your energy-producing reactions. More blood is diverted to your skin, so less blood (and therefore less oxygen) is getting to your muscles.

If it's humid, the humidity impacts the rate at which sweat can evaporate from your skin. This means your blood won't be cooled as much and is less effective at reducing your body temperature. Your body produces more sweat, further attempting to cool you down, which begins to dehydrate you, further impacting your performance.

★ In short, if you run in a hot, humid place at your usual effort level, you'll get hot quicker, sweat more, not be able to cool down very quickly and may become dehydrated. These will all limit your performance compared to your "usual" environment.

What about running at altitude?

There's less oxygen available (per volume of air) at altitude, which means that while you may not have quite as much blood being diverted to your skin, your blood will be carrying less oxygen, and less oxygen will be getting to your muscles – the impact is similar to running in heat.

★ In short, if you run at altitude at your usual effort level, you'll get less oxygen to your muscles, which will limit your performance compared to your typical environment.

How do heat, humidity and altitude impact your power metrics?

If you've been running max efforts in cooler, less humid conditions or at lower altitudes, when you run in hotter, more humid conditions or move to a higher altitude, your CP/FTP will be overstated for the hotter/more humid/higher altitude conditions.

★ This means that your workout targets will also be overstated. You may start to miss your targets and try even harder to achieve them, increasing your risk of injury ... all because of the impact of heat/humidity/altitude.

★ It also works the other way around – a CP/FTP set in a hot/humid/higher altitude environment will be understated if you run in cooler, less humid or lower altitude conditions. Your targets will start feeling easy, and you may miss out on potential performance improvements.

Is there a way to adjust your power numbers?

The Stryd team shared a Race Power Predictor modelled using Google Sheets. The calculation combines models from different research scientists into a single calculator that, given the power to convert (in Watts) along with pairs of values for temperature, humidity and altitude (representing the environment to convert from and the environment to convert to), returns a percentage and a converted power value.

The calculator has been built into [Stryd; Race Calculator (PowerCenter)] and [Stryd; Race Calculator (mobile)], allowing an event target calculated under one set of conditions to be converted to an event target under the conditions expected on the event day.

The Stryd team has also included the calculator logic in the Apple Watch app [Stryd; Workout app] and the Garmin datafield [Stryd; Stryd Zones]. Both of these support entry of baseline temperature, humidity, and altitude and will convert your real-time power based on real-time sensor readings of temperature, humidity, and altitude.

If you don't use a Stryd footpod, you can use [SPC for Sheets] to convert your workout or event targets from the environment conditions used to calculate them to the environment conditions forecast to be in place when you run your workout or event.

You can watch a YouTube video showing environmental conversions at [Palladino; Environmental conditions converter].

Treadmills

What's in this section?

Not all watches support treadmill running because they rely on GPS to calculate speed/distance.

★ You'll likely be running in a hotter, more humid environment than when running outside, which means your CP/FTP and your workout targets will be overstated. You may need to adjust your CP/FTP, workout targets, or weight setting to compensate.

★ Your Running Effectiveness may be impacted due to using different muscles and body movements than running outside or if you have inaccuracies in speed/distance due to the lack of GPS.

★ You will get different power numbers if running on a non-motorised treadmill (NMTM) compared to a motorised treadmill. In this case, you may need to determine an NMTM CP/FTP and use this to calculate training load metrics.

What's different about running on a treadmill?

Running on a treadmill presents a unique set of challenges:

- Many treadmills are in environments with high heat or humidity (often both).

- The treadmill motion looks like running, but it's a little different, as you're not moving yourself forward – instead, you're working to counteract the backwards-moving belt, which means your muscles are working slightly differently.

- Your running motion will be very regular (and constrained) compared to running outside, where you will be changing direction, handling kerbs or other changes in height, navigating uphills and downhills and (sometimes) having to battle the wind.

- Your power on a motorised treadmill will be different than your power (for the same effort) on a non-motorised treadmill.

- You might read (or be advised) to set the treadmill incline to 1% to match outdoor running at the same velocity. This is a generalisation, and the incline to use may be anywhere from 0%-1.5%, depending on your running speed.

- Some power meters can estimate your effort to overcome air resistance or a headwind. Air power is absent on a treadmill as you don't have to overcome air resistance, and the strongest gym fan isn't detectable as a headwind.

- Not all watches support treadmill running, as they rely on GPS to calculate speed/distance. If you're using a Stryd footpod, you can set your watch to take speed/distance from Stryd; if you're not, then as of the time of writing, only Garmin watches support speed/distance reporting on a treadmill, relying on a one-time calibration to be able to estimate your speed on the treadmill based on (I assume) comparison to your speed on previous outdoor runs.

It's possible to consider some of these impacts but not all.

Heat and humidity on a treadmill

Even with the strongest cool-air fans, it's very likely you'll be running in an environment with higher "local" humidity than when running outside – "local" humidity refers to the moisture immediately adjacent to your skin, as treadmill environments typically have little or no convectional cooling due to moving through air.

This means your CP/FTP will be overstated for the treadmill environment, and your power targets will also be overstated. You can use one of the calculators covered in the previous section to estimate the impact of the extra heat/humidity – there are three ways you can adjust to re-align everything:

1. Adjust your CP/FTP, which will, in turn, adjust your workout targets (as a percentage of CP/FTP). While this will ensure that your CP/FTP and workout targets are appropriate for the environment, adjusting your CP/FTP will take manual effort, and you'll need to remember to readjust when you next run outdoors. In addition, if you're using multiple planning or review apps, you may need to adjust each to ensure that your data aligns properly.

2. Leave your CP/FTP unchanged, but adjust your workout targets. This is easier than adjusting your CP/FTP, but it will make the workout look like it was run at a different power level than was intended by the original targets. Your actual effort may result in lower power numbers than the equivalent outdoor workout, affecting your training load or mix.

3. ☺ Adjust your weight, leaving your CP/FTP and workout targets unchanged. While this may seem strange, remember that your power meter uses your weight as a scaling factor, calculating your effort in Watts/kg and multiplying by your weight to show the result in Watts. Adjusting your weight scales up a lower effort (due to higher heat/humidity) so that your reported effort (in Watts) is on the same basis as your CP/FTP and workout targets, and your TSS/RSS can safely be included in your training load and other ongoing metrics.

Air power on a treadmill

If you're using a *[Stryd; Footpod]*, you may need to adjust for air power – the power used to overcome air resistance generated by your forward motion or running into a headwind.

Not all footpod versions report air power. Stryd introduced this feature with the Stryd Wind and has included it in subsequent models (Stryd NextGen and Stryd Duo).

Unfortunately, using a foot pod that reports air power means that your outdoor testing will include air power in calculating CP/FTP, while running on a treadmill will not (as there is no air resistance to overcome).

You can make several adjustments to compensate for the lack of air power. Steve Palladino's treadmill article *[Palladino; Using Running Power on the Treadmill]* covers these options in detail.

Motorised vs. non-motorised treadmill

An outdoor CP/FTP cannot be used on a non-motorised treadmill, nor can a motorised treadmill CP/FTP.

Why not?

From *[Palladino; Using Running Power on the Treadmill]*, "non-motorized treadmills have been noted to be associated with a significantly higher oxygen utilization, heart rate (HR) and rating of perceived exertion (RPE) compared to both motorized treadmill running and overground running".

If you're using a non-motorised treadmill, the best option may be to run a CP test on the treadmill, using the result to set workout targets (and adjusting your planning or reviewing tools appropriately).

Trails & Ultras

What's in this section?

Power is the best measure of intensity for trails and ultras, especially when combined with RPE.

★ You'll need four different power numbers, one each for Flat running, Uphill running, Uphill hiking, and Downhill running.

★ Max effort runs end CP test protocols only work for Flat running; for the other three, you'll need to use different test protocols, complete specific workouts and understand what your data shows.

I'm not a trail/ultra runner

I'll repeat it – I'm not a trail or ultra runner. I have little experience running these events and even less experience using power to run them.

There are some significant differences in how power can be used for those events compared to how it is used for track or road events.

What are the differences?

The Stryd team posted an excellent YouTube video featuring Andy Dubois, who runs an ultra/trail coaching business in Australia *[DuBois; Trail and ultra race planning]*.

In the video, Andy outlines the differences when Running with Power on trails and in ultras. In brief:

- Pace and Heart Rate are challenging to use in those environments; RPE is unreliable unless you're a very experienced trail/ultra runner; Power (as a measure of effort) is the best choice, especially when combined with RPE.

- You need four different power numbers, one each for Flat running, Uphill running, Uphill hiking, and Downhill running.

- The usual max effort runs and CP test protocols only work for Flat running; for the other three, you'll need to use different test protocols, and you'll need to spend time completing specific workouts and understanding what your data shows – understanding your data is critical if you're to have accurate numbers for all four.

☺ If you want to dive deeper into this topic, watch the video. You might also consider contacting Andy.

Chapter 9

Frequently Asked Questions (FAQ)

What's coming up?

This chapter answers frequently asked questions (FAQ) from runners new to power.

It provides brief answers and references to the chapters containing more information about the topic.

NOTE: The FAQ information was correct when this book was published but may now be outdated, given the speed with which Running with Power is evolving. If you have questions about whether an answer is still accurate, please ask in the [[f1r2a; Facebook Group]](.).

How is power measured when running?

Power is measured using a Power Meter. These small devices clip to your shoe, fit inside your shoe or attach to your torso or wrist. Many recent running watches include a built-in power meter.

The Power Meter models your movements and converts them into a power number shown on the watch or mobile app that you're using to view and record your power.

The power readings and the model used to convert them are specific to the Power Meter and watch/mobile app. If you run with two different Power Meters (even different generations of the same Power Meter), they will probably report different power numbers for the same run.

★ This means you should decide which Power Meter you will use and use it for every run. Mixing and matching isn't possible, and comparing readings from one power meter against those from another is pointless.

★ It also means there is no single "true" measure of the actual power used to run, but this doesn't matter as long as the Power Meter produces numbers that are repeatable (same effort under same conditions = same Power Number) and valid (aligned to your physiology).

Power Meters are covered in the **Getting Started** chapter.

How do I use the power numbers?

Power is a measure of intensity expressed in Watts. It may also be expressed in Watts/kg, which can be used to compare your ability to generate power against other runners or population averages.

★ Power models your effort – how hard you're running. If you increase your effort, the power number will increase; if you reduce your effort, the power number will decrease. This is true whether the change is because you decided to change it or due to the conditions, e.g. hills or wind.

★ The power readings from your workouts can be used to determine the Threshold (or, more accurately, the intensity range) above which you begin to fatigue more quickly. This, in turn, can be used to plan workout intensities, monitor your training load and set race-day targets.

Power numbers and your Threshold are covered in the **Fundamentals** chapter.

Is there a relationship between power and duration?

As anyone who's tried sprinting knows, there's an inverse relationship: higher power levels can be maintained for shorter durations; lower power levels can be maintained for longer durations.

The maximum power values that can be maintained for specific durations can be modelled as a Power-Duration Curve (PDC), with power on the vertical axis and duration on the horizontal.

The shape of the PDC will depend on the scale you're using for duration. If you're using a logarithmic scale, the curve will appear S-shaped (sigmoidal). If you're using a linear scale instead, the curve will appear hyperbolic (a curve with a bend in the middle).

★ Your PDC is individual to you and will change as you train or detrain – it reflects what you may be able to achieve based on your *current metabolic fitness*. It can be used to estimate your most likely performance at any duration on the modelled curve.

The relationship between power and duration and your PDC is covered in the **Power-Duration Curve** chapter.

What are CP and FTP?

Your Critical Power (CP) or Functional Threshold Power (FTP) provide the foundation for most other power metrics.

Monod and Scherrer define CP as "an exercise intensity that could be sustained for a very long time." Hill extended and validated the CP concept for whole-body exercise, noting that "for a very long time" was usually 30 to 60 minutes of exercise at CP.

FTP is a metric Andrew Coggan, PhD, developed. It is "the highest power that an athlete can maintain in a quasi-steady state without fatiguing." Steve Palladino applies this to running as "the highest power that a runner can maintain in a quasi-steady state without fatiguing, where the duration may range from 30-70 minutes, depending on the individual."

★ CP and FTP are measures of *your metabolic fitness* that can be determined using field-based testing (rather than lab-based testing) and that identify your Threshold – the narrow range of intensities below which you can sustain a steady effort for an extended period, and above which you begin to fatigue much more quickly and have to slow down or stop.

★ Your CP/FTP is used to plan workouts, monitor training load and set race-day targets.

Your CP/FTP is covered in the **Fundamentals** chapter.

How can I determine my CP/FTP?

★ There are many different protocols and models for estimating CP/FTP. Some are more valid (aligned to physiology) and, therefore, more useful than others.

The three most valid/useful are

1. A CP test – a single workout that includes two maximum effort sections, one short (typically 3 minutes) and one long (typically 10 minutes or more). The results from these maximum efforts can be used to calculate your CP.

2. Modelled FTP – a mathematical model based on maximum effort runs over a range of durations and implemented in the TrainingPeaks/WKO apps.

3. Auto-CP – modelled from maximum effort runs over a range of different durations and implemented in Stryd's PowerCenter.

Your CP/FTP can also be estimated from recent race data [*Palladino; Estimating FTP/CP from Race Power Data*], or if you've just started running or are returning from injury and can't yet manage maximum effort runs, you can use calculations based on easy runs to get a rough CP/FTP estimate [*Palladino; A method to roughly estimate FTP/CP*].

Methods for determining your CP/FTP are covered in the **Fundamentals** chapter.

How do I keep my CP/FTP updated?

CP/FTP is calculated using maximum efforts. As the name suggests, your maximum efforts are the highest power you can maintain for a specific duration.

The number of different durations included in the CP/FTP calculation depends on your choice of CP/FTP – a CP test has two maximum efforts, while modelled FTP and Auto-CP monitor your completed workouts to identify maximum efforts across a range of durations over the last 90 days.

★ This means that your training schedule should include regular CP tests or maximum effort runs, ideally at the start of a training cycle, every 4-6 weeks within a training cycle, and around two weeks before you run your goal event.

★ It's important that when using the modelled FTP or Auto-CP calculations, your maximum efforts should be executed under similar conditions to avoid variances from heat, humidity, altitude, wind, outdoor vs. treadmill, etc. Ideally, they should also be run over a flat route to prevent issues from hills.

Methods for maintaining an accurate CP/FTP are covered in the **Fundamentals** chapter.

Is my running CP/FTP the same as my cycling or swimming FTP?

There is no relationship between your running CP/FTP and your FTP in any other sport.

Each sport requires a different combination of body movements, and these differing combinations will result in differing metabolic demands.

Some sports rely on elastic energy return to supply part of the energy needed – a missing component from other sports.

Finally, different power meters model your power using different calculations and combinations of sensors – power readings from different power meters are not comparable.

★ If you are a multi-sport athlete, you should calculate CP/FTP separately for each sport.

Your CP/FTP is covered in the **Fundamentals** chapter.

Is CP/FTP the only metric I should monitor?

The five key metrics you should be familiar with and monitor when Running with Power are

1. CP/FTP. Your CP/FTP identifies a narrow range of intensities above which you begin to fatigue much more quickly. It represents your *current metabolic fitness* and is the foundation for many other metrics. See the **Fundamentals** chapter for more.

2. RE. Your Running Effectiveness measures how well you convert power to speed, enabling you to calculate a target power for a specific distance and to estimate your finish time (when combined with your Reserve Work Capacity or your Riegel Exponent). RE can also be used to monitor the results of improving your running (using plyometrics, drills or strength training). See the **Races & Events** chapter for more.

3. TSB/RSB. Your Training Stress Balance or Running Stress Balance indicates whether your training provides sufficient stress rather than too little or too much. The multi-step calculations include calculating two additional metrics: your Chronic Training Load (CTL)/42-day average, an indicator of longer-term changes in performance ability due to training stress to which your body may have adapted, and your Acute Training Load (ATL)/7-day average, an indicator of shorter-term changes

in performance ability due to training stress to which your body hasn't yet adapted. See the **Training** chapter for more.

4. Ramp Rate. Your ramp rate is the change in your CTL/42-day average over time and enables you to minimise injury risk, manage your training load progression, and plan a taper. See the **Training** and **Races & Events** chapters for more.

5. TID. Your Training Intensity Distribution (TID) provides insight into the composition and distribution of your training intensity, allowing you to monitor whether you're running at the mix of intensities appropriate for your goal event and your training plan stage. See the **Training** chapter for more.

How do I use power when planning training?

Different training intensities drive differing physiological and performance adaptations. This is no different for power than when using pace, heart rate or perceived exertion.

What is different with power is that:

- target intensities can be based on your CP/FTP, individualising your training intensity to match your current fitness and building in progression as your CP/FTP improves

- higher-intensity interval targets can be based on your CP/FTP and Reserve Work Capacity (RWC), which varies from individual to individual and is a key metric for intensities above CP/FTP. [*Palladino; Interval Power Target Calculator*] calculates higher-intensity interval targets.

- your training plan should include CP tests or max effort runs so that you maintain (and check) your CP/FTP as a part of your training

- you can choose a training plan based on your current ability using your CP/FTP (in Watts/kg) – plans for higher abilities may contain more runs per week (and perhaps double-run days), as well as a different mix of intensities and longer durations

Training is covered in the **Training** chapter.

How can I set power-based workout targets?

Power enables you to use more precise training targets. Targets can be set using percentages based on your CP/FTP and are often quite narrow compared to plans based on pace or heart rate (for example, intervals at 98%-100% of CP/FTP, compared with pace or heart rate targets that might equate to 95%-105% of CP/FTP).

Why would you want narrow targets based on CP/FTP?

★ Training stimulates the adaptations appropriate for your goal event (e.g. increased heart stroke volume, increased muscle glycogen storage, adjustments to muscle fibre types). Those adaptations often need a precise training stress. Or, the range of intensities that produce a particular adaptation might be wider, but you have more chance of hitting the right intensity if you can target the middle of the range (rather than being on the high or low side).

★ Being able to target relatively narrow ranges also offers more opportunities for a mix of workout types, providing more workout variety while promoting the targeted adaptations.

Training targets are covered in the **Training** chapter.

Can I use power to monitor my training load?

There are three different elements you should be monitoring when training:

- ★ Your training load. So that your balance between shorter-term fatigue and longer-term adaptations is productive – that you're not under-training or over-training.

- ★ Your Ramp Rate. To minimise injury risk, manage your training load progression, and plan a taper.

- ★ Your mix of intensities. So that it's appropriate for your goal event and aligned with where you are in your training plan.

Training with Power assigns a Stress Score (TSS/RSS) to each workout, then combines the scores from multiple workouts into a Stress Balance (TSB/RSB), which can be used to monitor whether your training is productive, if it's not providing enough training stress, or if you're at risk of over-training or injury.

Stress Scores are also used to calculate your Ramp Rate, which can be used to monitor how quickly you're adding or removing training load, minimise injury risk, manage your training load progression, and plan a taper.

To monitor your mix of intensities, you can monitor your Training Intensity Distribution (TID), which shows your week-by-week relative mix of intensities as a percentage of total time training and your volume at each intensity, shown as hours.

★ These metrics can be applied to workouts you've completed. They can also be used with your upcoming workouts to plan your training progression or to plan a taper as you approach your goal event – the calculations for both are very similar.

Training load and intensity distribution are covered in the **Training** chapter.

How can I set race/event targets?

You can set race/event targets based on your CP/FTP (your individual metabolic fitness).

The simplest way to do this is as a percentage of CP/FTP – for example, "most runners run a 10k at around 100-104% of their CP/FTP" or "most runners run a marathon at around 91-94% of their CP/FTP". This method is not individualised and may not be accurate for every runner.

If you use a Stryd footpod, the Stryd Race Planner can provide a more accurate target race power. However, it's unclear whether it uses your Reserve Work Capacity (RWC) for shorter events, which can mean the prediction may lose accuracy.

If you want full control over the inputs and the calculation method, Super-Power Calculator for Sheets can model best-case, worst-case, and most likely scenarios for shorter events using your RWC and for longer events using your Riegel Exponent.

★ All methods depend on an accurate and recent CP/FTP and information about your Running Effectiveness. Depending on the model, you must also know your RWC or your Riegel Exponent.

Race/event targets are covered in the **Races & Events** chapter.

Power doesn't tell me what time I might achieve – what does?

★ Your Running Effectiveness (RE) measures how effectively you convert power into speed.

RE can be used:

- to estimate time from planned power and distance or to estimate the power needed to finish a race in a goal time

- as an indicator of fatigue (higher RE at the start of a workout, lower at the end) and as a way to track workout improvements over time

- to assess the impact of working on your form – if you're working on your form (perhaps using drills or plyometrics), you can use RE to gauge whether you're becoming more effective at converting power to speed (or less effective!)

- to compare runners – the RE values for different runners can be used to gauge who might have the greater potential for higher speed

- to compare shoes – it's possible to measure RE for different shoes to see which produces a higher RE (and would enable you to run faster for the same effort)

Running Effectiveness is covered in the **Races & Events** chapter.

Can I Run with Power on a treadmill?

Maybe, as long as you take specific differences into account:

- Not all watches support treadmill running as they rely on GPS to calculate speed/distance. Using a Stryd footpod, you can set your watch to take speed/distance from Stryd. If not, only Garmin watches support speed/distance reporting on a treadmill.

- You'll be running in a hotter, more humid environment than running outside, which means your CP/FTP and power targets may be overstated. You may need to adjust your CP/FTP, workout targets, or weight setting.

- Running Effectiveness. Treadmill running uses different movements than running outside (you're counteracting the movement of the belt rather than moving yourself forward), which may affect the power reported by your power meter. If you also have inaccuracies in speed/distance (few treadmills display speed accurately), both will impact your RE.

- Non-motorised treadmill. Running on a non-motorised treadmill will give different power numbers than a motorised treadmill. You may need to run a CP test on the treadmill, using the resulting CP/FTP to set workout targets.

Power on treadmills is covered in the **Environments** chapter.

Can I Run with Power on trails or ultras?

There are some significant differences in how to use power for those events compared to how to use power for track or road events:

- pace and heart rate are difficult to use in those environments; Rate of Perceived Exertion (RPE) is unreliable unless you're a very experienced trail/ultra runner; Power (as a measure of effort) is the best choice, especially when combined with RPE

- you need four different power numbers, one each for Flat running, Uphill running, Uphill hiking, and Downhill running

- the usual max effort runs or test protocols only work for Flat running; for the other three, you'll need to use different test protocols, and you'll need to spend time completing specific workouts and understanding what your data shows – understanding your data is critical if you're to have accurate numbers for all four

Power on trails or ultras is covered in the **Environments** chapter.

How can I keep track of all this "stuff"?

You'll need to choose some apps – at a minimum, somewhere to plan your workouts and somewhere to review your results.

There are many choices, and more become available each month. The difficulty is that your app choices interact with your choice of power meter and watch – a decision for one almost always has implications for the others.

You can take a couple of different approaches when deciding which apps to use:

1. Choose a popular combination. If you don't want to spend time evaluating options, you can choose one of the popular combinations – the Stryd ecosystem or TrainingPeaks / WKO.

2. Choose your own combination. If you prefer to evaluate options and make up your own mind, you can use the criteria presented in the **Getting Started** chapter as a starting point for your evaluation.

Your options for keeping track of "stuff" are covered in the **Getting Started** chapter.

Where can I find power-based training plans?

Several different options are available for you to create your own power-based workouts and training plans, and they are outlined in the **Getting Started** chapter.

If instead, you want to purchase a power-based training plan:

- If you use the Stryd ecosystem, *[Stryd; Training Plans]* contains various plans for Running with Power.

- *[Final Surge; Training Plans]* has a good selection of power-based plans – search for "power".

- *[TrainingPeaks; Training Plans]* has a good selection of plans. The link searches for plans with "power" in the description.

There are many others (and I'm sure there will be many more) as Running with Power's popularity continues to grow.

The **Training** chapter contains criteria that can be used to develop your own workouts/plans, or to assess whether a plan you're about to buy (or embark on) fully supports Running with Power.

Where can I find coaches who Coach with Power?

Here are some of the places you can find power-aware coaches:

- If you use the Stryd ecosystem *[Stryd; Coaches]* lists coaches that coach using the Stryd footpod

- TrainingPeaks has a large register of coaches *[TrainingPeaks; Coach Search]*, many of whom coach Running with Power

When searching for a coach, don't just focus on what they know about Running with Power.

Look at their certifications or qualifications – have they been trained to coach runners?

Ask about references from other runners they're coaching or have coached.

And ask to meet them virtually or in person. Only once you've met a coach can you decide whether you want to enter into a coaching relationship with them. It *is* a relationship, with you and your coach working together to improve your running or train you for an event – so it's worth finding out if you'll get along.

I have more questions ... where can I ask them?

Facebook is a great place for your questions, as you'll not only get answers (from a variety of different runners) but may also benefit from related discussions. You can also search to see if anyone has asked your question before.

Why not try the following Facebook groups:

- from1runner2another [f1r2a; Facebook Group] – if you have specific questions on content in this book, ask them in this group. The group is an excellent place for any other running-related questions.

- Palladino Power Project [Palladino; PPP Facebook group] – Steve offers advice on anything related to Running with Power, answers questions about his training plans and may provide race/event planning support (depending on his other commitments). Steve also offers the superb [Palladino; A Compendium of Race Power Planning Resources], a great resource he continues expanding and refining.

- Stryd Community [Stryd; Facebook group] – If you have questions about your Stryd footpod or the Stryd ecosystem, this is the place to ask them. The Stryd team is usually quick to answer, and if your question is better handled by their support team, they can point you in the right direction.

Glossary

ATL - [Acute Training Load](#)
>Originated by Andrew Coggan, PhD, ATL models the shorter-term impacts of your training and is a relative indicator of changes in your performance potential from training load to which you haven't yet adapted.
>See the **Training** chapter for more information.

Auto-CP - [Auto-calculated Critical Power](#)
>A part of the Stryd ecosystem that automatically calculates your Critical Power (CP) from your last 90 days of training data.
>See the **Fundamentals** chapter for more information.

CP - Critical Power
> The highest intensity that can be sustained while maintaining a steady(ish) metabolic state. CP is a measure of your metabolic fitness. When training, you can track changes in your CP by regularly re-testing.
> See the **Fundamentals** chapter for more information.

CP/FTP - Critical Power/Functional Threshold Power
> Critical Power (CP) and Functional Threshold Power (FTP) while calculated differently, reflect similar physiologic states and are used interchangeably when running with power. They are a field-based way of identifying the phase transition from heavy to sever intensities.
> See the **Fundamentals** chapter for more information.

CTL - Chronic Training Load
> Originated by Andrew Coggan, PhD, CTL models the longer-term impacts of your training and is a relative indicator of changes in your performance potential from training load to which you may have adapted.
> See the **Training** chapter for more information.

detraining - [Detraining](#)
> The partial or complete loss of training-induced anatomical, physiological and performance adaptations, as a consequence of training reduction or cessation.
> See the **Training** chapter for more information.

FTP - [Functional Threshold Power](#)
> A term defined by Andrew Coggan, PhD, FTP is the highest power that can be maintained in a quasi-steady state without fatiguing.
> See the **Fundamentals** chapter for more information.

Head Unit - [Head Unit](#)
> A device used to record sensor data while you workout: most commonly a watch or band or sometimes a smartphone-based App. Most head units will connect to multiple sensors using Bluetooth or ANT+ and consolidate the sensor data into a FIT file.
> See the **Getting Started** chapter for more information.

HR - Heart Rate
> The number of times your heart beats in a minute. If you're following a training plan based on HR, each workout should target HR Zones that you aim for as you exercise (increasing your effort if below the zone, or decreasing if above). Heart Rate is one way to calibrate your training and racing, the others being Pace, Power and RPE.
> See the **Why Run with Power?** chapter for more information.

MLSS - Maximal Lactate Steady State
> The maximum intensity at which lactate concentration remains in quasi-steady state. MLSS can be used to identify the phase transition from heavy to severe intensities, but relies on blood testing while running 2, 3 or more 30 minute exercise bouts. When running with power, CP/FTP is a field-based way of determining the phase transition.
> See the **Fundamentals** chapter for more information.

MMP - Mean-Max Power Curve
> A chart of the maximum power you've achieved for multiple durations, usually calculated from workouts completed in the last 90 days. Your Mean-Max Power Curve shows what you have achieved.
> See the **Power-Duration Curve** chapter for more information.

Pace - Pace
> The speed with which you're running, expressed as the number of minutes to complete a kilometre or mile (e.g. 6 min/km). If you're following a training plan based on Pace, each workout should target specific pace ranges or pace zones that you aim for as you exercise (increasing your effort if slower than target pace, or decreasing if faster). Pace is one way to calibrate your training and racing, the others being Heart Rate, Power and RPE.
> See the **Why Run with Power?** chapter for more information.

PDC - Power-Duration Curve
> A "line of best fit" through the highs and lows of your MMP Curve, or across the highs of your MMP Curve. Your Power-Duration Curve shows what you could achieve.
> See the **Power-Duration Curve** chapter for more information.

phase transition - phase transition
> A narrow domain, in which there is a gradual move from one state to another (rather than a sudden switchover). The phase transition indicated by CP/FTP is important for runners.
> See the **Fundamentals** chapter for more information.

Ramp Rate - [Ramp Rate](#)
> Measures changes in your training load, enabling you to assess how quickly you're adding load (so that you can reduce your risk of injury), and how quickly you're removing load (to plan a taper leading up to your event).
> See the **Training** chapter for more information.

RE - [Running Effectiveness](#)
> Measures how effectively a runner converts power to speed (a speed:power ratio). Not to be confused with Running Economy (a lab-based metric using oxygen consumption) or Running Efficiency (based on external mechanical power vs. metabolic power production).
> See the **Races & Events** chapter for more information.

Riegel Exponent - Riegel Exponent
> The Riegel formula was originally developed to predict race times based on performances at other distances. It models the relationship between speed and distance. The formula produces an exponential curve, with the shape of the curve dependent on the exponent value. Your Riegel Exponent is important for events where your effort is below CP/FTP (e.g. 15k, half marathon, full marathon), and can be used to estimate your finish time for that longer event.
> See the **Power-Duration Curve** chapter for more information.

RPE - Rating of Perceived Exertion
> A method for assessing perceived exertion during exercise, as measured by a Borg rating of perceived exertion scale.
> See the **Why Run with Power?** chapter for more information.

RSB - Running Stress Balance
> Originated by the Stryd team, RSB compares your historic training to your recent training and is calculated using weighted averages based on your workout RSS scores
> See the **Training** chapter for more information.

RSS - [Running Stress Score](#)
> Originated by the Stryd team, RSS is a method for assigning a score to a run that takes into account the duration and the intensity, plus a coefficient reflecting the higher stressing effect of intensive run workouts.
> See the **Training** chapter for more information.

RWC - [Reserve Work Capacity](#)
> Reserve Work Capacity (RWC) is the amount of work you can do above CP/FTP where Work = Power * Duration. RWC is important for events where your effort is above CP/FTP (e.g. 3k, 5k), and can be used to estimate your finish time for that shorter event.
> See the **Power-Duration Curve** chapter for more information.

Tapering - [Tapering](#)
> A planned reduction in exercise in the days just before an important event. Tapering aims to balance the loss of training time against the time needed to recover from recent training fatigue, so that you arrive at the start line for your event "on fresh legs".
> See the **Races & Events** chapter for more information.

Threshold - [shorthand for phase transition](#)
> The phase transition indicated by CP/FTP - see "phase transition".
> See the **Fundamentals** chapter for more information.

TID - [Training Intensity Distribution](#)
> Tracks time spent at various intensities so that you can monitor whether you're running at the mix of intensities appropriate for your goal event and your training plan stage.
> See the **Training** chapter for more information.

Training load - [Training Load](#)
> Training Stress accumulated via repeated training bouts. If you increase your training load too quickly (if your ramp rate is too high), you'll increase your risk of injury.
> See the **Training** chapter for more information.

Training progression - [Training Progression](#)
> Gradually increasing your training volume by increasing the duration of your long runs, adding extra intervals or reducing your recovery time between intervals.
> See the **Training** chapter for more information.

TSB - [Training Stress Balance](#)
> Originated by Andrew Coggan, PhD, TSB compares your historic training to your recent training and is calculated as CTL minus ATL.
> See the **Training** chapter for more information.

TSS - [Training Stress Score](#)
> Originated by Andrew Coggan, PhD, TSS is a method for assigning a score to a run that takes into account the duration and the intensity. TSS is used to calculate ATL, CTL and TSB, and is a registered trademark of Peaksware.
> See the **Training** chapter for more information.

TTE - [Time To Exhaustion](#)
> Originated by Andrew Coggan, PhD, TTE is the maximum duration for which you can hold your FTP. This is typically somewhere between 30 and 70 minutes.
> See the **Power-Duration Curve** chapter for more information.

VO2max - [Maximum Volume of Oxygen consumption](#)
> The maximum rate of oxygen utilisation attainable during physical exertion. When running with power, VO2max is a less useful measure than CP/FTP.
> See the **Fundamentals** chapter for more information.

Bibliography

Allen, Coggan & McGregor; Functional Reserve Capacity
Allen, H., Coggan, A. & McGregor, S., (2019) Training+Racing with a Power Meter, 3rd Edition (pp. 145-146). Boulder: Velopress.

Allen, Coggan & McGregor; Functional Threshold Power
Allen, H., Coggan, A. & McGregor, S., (2019) Training+Racing with a Power Meter, 3rd Edition (pp. 147-148). Boulder: Velopress.

Allen, Coggan & McGregor; Impulse-Response Model
Allen, H., Coggan, A. & McGregor, S., (2019) Training+Racing with a Power Meter, 3rd Edition (pp. 153-154). Boulder: Velopress.

Allen, Coggan & McGregor; Performance Manager
Allen, H., Coggan, A. & McGregor, S., (2019) Training+Racing with a Power Meter, 3rd Edition (pp. 158-160). Boulder: Velopress.

Allen, Coggan & McGregor; Power Duration Curve
Allen, H., Coggan, A. & McGregor, S., (2019) Training+Racing with a Power Meter, 3rd Edition (pp. 48-51). Boulder: Velopress.

Allen, Coggan & McGregor; Time To Exhaustion
Allen, H., Coggan, A. & McGregor, S., (2019) Training+Racing with a Power Meter, 3rd Edition (pp. 148-149). Boulder: Velopress.

Allen, Coggan & McGregor; Training Stress Score
Allen, H., Coggan, A. & McGregor, S., (2019) Training+Racing with a Power Meter, 3rd Edition (pp. 112-114). Boulder: Velopress.

Apple; Watch
Shop Apple Watch
Available at:
https://www.apple.com/uk/shop/buy-watch
(Accessed 16 Mar 2024)

Banister; Impulse-Response Model
Calvert, T.W., Banister, E.W., Savage, M.V., Bach, T., (1976) A Systems Model of the Effects of Training on Physical Performance
Available at:
https://ieeexplore.ieee.org/document/5409179 (Accessed 16 Mar 2024)

Burnley; Exercise intensity domains and phase transitions

Burnley, M., (2020) Exercise intensity domains and phase transitions: the power-duration relationship
Available at: https://drmarkburnley.wordpress.com/2020/08/31/exercise-intensity-domains-and-phase-transitions-the-power-duration-relationship/ (Accessed 16 Mar 2024)

Cerezuela-Espejo et al.; Are we ready to measure running power?

Cerezuela-Espejo, V. et al., (2020) Are we ready to measure running power? Repeatability and concurrent validity of five commercial technologies. National Library of Medicine.
Available at: https://pubmed.ncbi.nlm.nih.gov/32212955/ (Accessed 16 Mar 2024)

Coggan; Cycling Power Zones

Coggan, A., Cycling Power Zones Explained
Available at: https://www.trainingpeaks.com/blog/power-training-levels/ (Accessed 16 Mar 2024)

Coggan; WKO4: New Metrics for Running With Power

Coggan, A., WKO4: New Metrics for Running With Power
Available at: https://www.trainingpeaks.com/blog/wko4-new-metrics-for-running-with-power/ (Accessed 16 Mar 2024)

compared to

compared to

Coros; Watch

Coros GPS Watches
Available at: https://uk.coros.com/watches (Accessed 16 Mar 2024)

DuBois; Trail and ultra race planning

Duboid, A., (2018) Trail and ultra race planning with Andy DuBois - hosted by Stryd on YouTube
Available at: https://www.youtube.com/watch?v=29UE7khUoS4 (Accessed 16 Mar 2024)

Elevate

Elevate for Strava
Available at: https://thomaschampagne.github.io/elevate/ (Accessed 16 Mar 2024)

Empirical Cycling; Podcast

Empirical Cycling Podcast
Available at: https://www.empiricalcycling.com/podcast.html (Accessed 16 Mar 2024)

f1r2a; Facebook Group
Facebook Group: from1runner2another
Available at:
https://www.facebook.com/groups/from1runner2another (Accessed 16 Mar 2024)

Fellrnr; Practical Tapering
Practical Tapering
Available at:
https://fellrnr.com/wiki/Practical_Tapering (Accessed 16 Mar 2024)

Final Surge
Final Surge - Train and Coach with a Purpose
Available at: https://www.finalsurge.com/ (Accessed 16 Mar 2024)

Final Surge; Beta platform
Final Surge - Beta platform
Available at:
https://beta.finalsurge.com/workoutcalendar (Accessed 16 Mar 2024)

Final Surge; Training Plans
Final Surge - Training Plans for Every Goal
Available at:
https://www.finalsurge.com/trainingplans (Accessed 16 Mar 2024)

Garmin; HRM
Garmin Heart Rate Monitors
Available at: https://www.garmin.com/en-GB/c/heart-rate-monitors/ (Accessed 16 Mar 2024)

Garmin; Running Dynamics Pod
Garmin Running Dynamics Pod
Available at: https://www.garmin.com/en-GB/p/561205 (Accessed 16 Mar 2024)

Garmin; Running Power datafield
Running Power datafield
Available at: https://apps.garmin.com/en-US/apps/741afa11-0250-48e2-86b5-14bd47e29391 (Accessed 16 Mar 2024)

Garmin; RunPowerModel datafield
RunPowerModel datafield
Available at: https://apps.garmin.com/en-US/apps/6ac39398-29fa-4183-a9ac-8396ce941446 (Accessed 16 Mar 2024)

Garmin; RunPowerWorkout datafield
RunPowerWorkout datafield
Available at: https://apps.garmin.com/en-US/apps/8c2fce29-0c7c-41f3-9a8f-5d3093c9cf2f (Accessed 16 Mar 2024)

Garmin; Watch
Garmin Running Smartwatches
Available at: https://www.garmin.com/en-GB/c/sports-fitness/running-smartwatches/ (Accessed 16 Mar 2024)

Golden Cheetah
Golden Cheetah
Available at: https://www.goldencheetah.org/ (Accessed 16 Mar 2024)

Hill; The Critical Power Concept
Hill, D., (2012) The Critical Power Concept
Available at:
https://link.springer.com/article/10.2165/00007256-199316040-00003 (Accessed 16 Mar 2024)

intervals.icu
Intervals.icu
Available at: https://intervals.icu/ (Accessed 16 Mar 2024)

iSmoothRun
iSmoothRun - Run farther, Run faster, Train smarter
Available at: http://www.ismoothrun.com/ (Accessed 16 Mar 2024)

Jack Daniels; VDOT
V.O2 running calculator
Available at: https://vdoto2.com/calculator/ (Accessed 16 Mar 2024)

Markus Holler; RunPowerModel datafield
RunPowerModel datafield
Available at: https://apps.garmin.com/en-US/apps/6ac39398-29fa-4183-a9ac-8396ce941446 (Accessed 16 Mar 2024)

Maturana et al.; Critical power: How different protocols and models affect its determination
Maturana, F.M., Fontana, F.Y., Pogliaghi, S., Passfield, L., Murias, J.M., (2017) Critical power: How different protocols and models affect its determination
Available at: https://www.jsams.org/article/S1440-2440(17)31817-0/fulltext (Accessed 16 Mar 2024)

Monod and Scherrer; The Work Capacity of a Synergic Muscular Group
Monod, H. & Scherrer, J., (2007) The Work Capacity of a Synergic Muscle Group
Available at: https://www.tandfonline.com/doi/abs/10.1080/00140136508930810 (Accessed 16 Mar 2024)

Mujika and Padilla; Detraining - Part I (short-term)
Mujika, I., Padilla, S., (2012) Detraining: Loss of Training-Induced Physiological and Performance Adaptations. Part I
Available at: https://link.springer.com/article/10.2165/00007256-200030020-00002 (Accessed 16 Mar 2024)

Mujika and Padilla; Detraining - Part II (long-term)

Mujika, I., Padilla, S., (2012) Detraining: Loss of Training-Induced Physiological and Performance Adaptations. Part II
Available at:
https://link.springer.com/article/10.2165/00007256-200030030-00001 (Accessed 16 Mar 2024)

Palladino; A Compendium of Race Power Planning Resources

Palladino, S., (2019) A Compendium of Race Power Planning Resources
Available at:
https://docs.google.com/document/d/e/2PACX-1vR26MjsQnC08GiCnT71kIcvCajtkeKiADLLb7DR75S9n0rk4ymqtEz4mKI8tgcGSXpfnxvGW6_N_5rm/pub (Accessed 16 Mar 2024)

Palladino; A method to roughly estimate FTP/CP

Palladino, A., (2021) A method to roughly estimate FTP/CP for runners not ready to properly test.
Available at:
https://docs.google.com/document/d/e/2PACX-1vR8wNT_OF3TCF0MsM3ixnXtoKaQGNvyQ94mnnNLe2ujdwM5tTTHcfFyszDtFx2ZJlTxC0Kyyh-4pQs9/pub (Accessed 16 Mar 2024)

Palladino; Article library
>Palladino, S., Article library
>Available at:
>https://docs.google.com/document/u/1/d/e/2PACX-1vRwRFiXs6hJgygdwyzT33sDis7a70bICb2kymTs12GhhtkZi_vO5bJdzu-RUTR6953uKPbHSeR2H1yy/pub (Accessed 16 Mar 2024)

Palladino; Environmental conditions converter
>Palladino, S., (2020) Youtube - Demonstration of the SPC v4 environmental conditions converter
>Available at:
>https://www.youtube.com/watch?v=nmpA03f7OR4&list=PLn_-H5VMWQwWWId6LmXf0nddXULASaKfD&index=20 (Accessed 16 Mar 2024)

Palladino; Estimating FTP/CP from Race Power Data
>Palladino, S., (2019) Estimating FTP/CP from Race Power Data
>Available at:
>https://docs.google.com/document/d/e/2PACX-1vQ7ytxwRThXaQCbyJhmYpiH2k3EPUDvqQGwEsh-NZBlOaBtzcTaJkarL_T9uSyXDNf-9wOOqrYj2nFQ/pub (Accessed 16 Mar 2024)

Palladino; How does Stryd Auto-CP work?
Palladino, S., (2020) How does Stryd Auto-CP work?
Available at:
https://docs.google.com/document/d/e/2PACX-1vRBe-k5GiCz1Vqj9W25PxiAkLY1OffKM6k4EjcGy0JIFNC7ibNEcOUIpm2b3lANnJ5Rz-6GtmcemOfz/pub (Accessed 16 Mar 2024)

Palladino; Interval Power Target Calculator
Final Surge Beta Platform: Palladino Power Project - Interval Power Target Calculator
Available at:
https://beta.finalsurge.com/workoutcalendar (Accessed 16 Mar 2024)

Palladino; PPP Facebook group
Facebook - Palladino Power Project
Available at:
https://www.facebook.com/groups/PalladinoPowerProject (Accessed 16 Mar 2024)

Palladino; Protocol for CP testing
Palladino, S., (2020) Protocol for CP Testing
Available at:
https://docs.google.com/document/d/e/2PACX-1vTCQxo18-LsfWt1gnHyEJ0nUccxhWhJAMzaS9qmWpvoBGqcuC4vpO08fbn2zA8jD_G1S2eHtlPFlEo1/pub (Accessed 16 Mar 2024)

Palladino; Race Planning using Riegel Exponents and RE

Palladino, S., (2020) YouTube - Basic use of the 'Generate Race Power Scenarios using pairs of Riegel Exponents and RE' function
Available at:
https://www.youtube.com/watch?v=5kSWzSC03zk&list=PLn_-H5VMWQwWWId6LmXf0nddXULASaKfD&index=16 (Accessed 16 Mar 2024)

Palladino; Race Planning using RWC and RE

Palladino, S., (2020) YouTube - Race Power Planning with SuperPower Calculator v4 - using FTP/CP, RWC, and Running Effectiveness
Available at:
https://www.youtube.com/watch?v=3LRECH3cvbk&list=PLn_-H5VMWQwWWId6LmXf0nddXULASaKfD&index=18 (Accessed 16 Mar 2024)

Palladino; Race power as a percentage of FTP/CP

Palladino, S., (2023) Race power as a percentage of FTP/CP
Available at:
https://docs.google.com/document/d/e/2PACX-1vTFVyUW6fuohdZrGr5VTNvBT16jkUr-8EUnh8IjRax8dEhnTC8kfpUXwsInO1_YUSf4ezgRwKz3kSbY/pub (Accessed 16 Mar 2024)

Palladino; Reserve Work Capacity
Palladino, S., (2020) The size of one's RWC
Available at:
https://www.facebook.com/groups/PalladinoPowerProject/posts/2851710825080955/
(Accessed 16 Mar 2024)

Palladino; Running FTP - A Primer
Palladino, S., (2017) Running Functional Threshold Power - A Primer
Available at:
https://docs.google.com/document/d/e/2PACX-1vT2ucrcwUlitpfi6qFkU9URQSy5GVBQknsKvLf7iLDJBqW7g-jc3k01JkygYib7YhoWK874Q9fWKlt_/pub
(Accessed 16 Mar 2024)

Palladino; Running Power Zones
Palladino, S., (2017) Running Power Zones
Available at:
https://docs.google.com/document/d/e/2PACX-1vTHqzlWwp2Dp6f1cMlS45PycEf-hCAjy61KXG7fRoR2e4mxDyWH6gXo5Znlvj5b9cTBWBcj9kcfJHel/pub (Accessed 16 Mar 2024)

Palladino; Understanding and Applying CP Testing for Runners
Palladino, S., (2020) Understanding and Applying CP Testing for Runners
Available at: https://docs.google.com/document/d/e/2PACX-1vSz0ryPMD4vVJLi2HGjkqoUKRzRPhN78TUNlCmuYcrLTjeLPx-ZaiROk9NG96iatJ4zYKAQcbjEEot0/pub (Accessed 16 Mar 2024)

Palladino; Understanding 'Running Effectiveness' and its uses
Palladino, S., (2017) Understanding 'Running Effectiveness' and its uses
Available at: https://docs.google.com/document/d/e/2PACX-1vTzjH-Ns_GlnUm4lAxi3cVOQpzzKcWNF6VEX271s-QGYFHjwMgyLhhmu5i21-1_CaC3eL0B817rQo8k/pub (Accessed 16 Mar 2024)

Palladino; Using Running Power on the Treadmill
Palladino, S., (2020) Using Running Power on the Treadmill
Available at: https://docs.google.com/document/d/e/2PACX-1vTeJhTbZkL7XsVUK7k8hNtUPtWRrMfq4flKJK0Q_vKDiOd4qT14aw_AzDBZTcFTq-mumpdOss4Ejv1O/pub (Accessed 16 Mar 2024)

Polar; Watch
Polar Vantage V Series
Available at: https://www.polar.com/uk-en/running-watches/ (Accessed 16 Mar 2024)

Riegel; Athletic Records and Human Endurance
Riegel, P., (1981) Athletic Records and Human Endurance: A time vs. distance equation describing world-record performances may be used to compare the relative endurance capabilities of various groups of people.
Available at: https://www.jstor.org/stable/27850427 (Accessed 16 Mar 2024)

Rowbottom; SFRA model
Rowbottom, D. (2000) Periodization of training. Exercise and Sport Science, 499–512.

RPM2; Footbed Power Meter
Remote Performance Measurement/Monitoring
Available at: https://www.rpm2.com/ (Accessed 16 Mar 2024)

SPC for Sheets
Make a copy of: SuperPower Calculator for Sheets (SPCs)
Available at: https://f1r2a.com/SuperPower_Calculator (Accessed 16 Mar 2024)

SPC for Web
SuperPower Calculator for Web (SPCw)
Available at:
https://superpowercalculator.com/
(Accessed 16 Mar 2024)

Sport Tracks
Sport Tracks
Available at: https://sporttracks.mobi/
(Accessed 16 Mar 2024)

Stryd; Auto-CP
Introducing auto-calculated Critical Power: Accelerate your improvements by running in the perfect power zone.
Available at:
https://blog.stryd.com/2019/07/09/introducing-auto-calculated-critical-power/
(Accessed 16 Mar 2024)

Stryd; Coaches
Stryd Coaches
Available at:
https://buy.stryd.com/uk/en/coaches
(Accessed 16 Mar 2024)

Stryd; Connecting to TrainingPeaks
How to manually import structured workouts to your Apple Watch or Garmin from TrainingPeaks
Available at:
https://help.stryd.com/en/articles/8926985-trainingpeaks-and-stryd (Accessed 16 Mar 2024)

Stryd; Facebook group
Stryd Facebook group
Available at: https://www.facebook.com/groups/strydcommunity (Accessed 16 Mar 2024)

Stryd; Footpod
Stryd Footpod
Available at: https://www.stryd.com/ (Accessed 16 Mar 2024)

Stryd; How RSS differs from TSS
What is the RSS and how does it differ from TSS?
Available at: https://help.stryd.com/en/articles/6879537-what-is-the-rss-and-how-does-it-differ-from-tss (Accessed 16 Mar 2024)

Stryd; Membership
Stryd Membership
Available at: https://buy.stryd.com/us/en/pages/membership (Accessed 16 Mar 2024)

Stryd; Mobile app
Stryd Mobile App
Available at: https://www.stryd.com/uk/en/mobile (Accessed 16 Mar 2024)

Stryd; PowerCenter
Stryd PowerCenter
Available at: https://www.stryd.com/powercenter (Accessed 16 Mar 2024)

Stryd; Race Calculator
Race Calculator

Stryd; Race Calculator (mobile)
Stryd Race Power Calculator and Event Planner (mobile)
Available at:
https://help.stryd.com/en/articles/6879548-race-calculator-and-event-planner-on-mobile (Accessed 16 Mar 2024)

Stryd; Race Calculator (PowerCenter)
Stryd Race Power Calculator
Available at:
https://help.stryd.com/en/articles/6879547-race-power-calculator (Accessed 16 Mar 2024)

Stryd; Race Calculator requirements
Stryd Race Power Calculator Requirements
Available at:
https://help.stryd.com/en/articles/6879547-race-power-calculator-requirements (Accessed 16 Mar 2024)

Stryd; Running Stress Balance
Stryd Running Stress Balance
Available at:
https://help.stryd.com/en/articles/6879346-running-stress-balance (Accessed 16 Mar 2024)

Stryd; Running Stress Score
Stryd Running Stress Score
Available at: https://blog.stryd.com/2017/01/28/running-stress-score/ (Accessed 16 Mar 2024)

Stryd; Stryd Zones
Stryd Zones | Data Field (for Garmin Watches)
Available at: https://apps.garmin.com/en-US/apps/18fb2cf0-1a4b-430d-ad66-988c847421f4 (Accessed 16 Mar 2024)

Stryd; Stryd Zones Data Fields and Garmin Watch Setup
Stryd Zones Data Fields and Garmin Watch Setup with Stryd and Stryd Duo
Available at: https://help.stryd.com/en/articles/8594075-stryd-zones-data-fields-and-garmin-watch-setup-with-stryd-and-stryd-duo (Accessed 16 Mar 2024)

Stryd; Training for Your 5K Personal Best
Stryd Training for Your 5K Personal Best
Available at: https://blog.stryd.com/2021/08/04/training-for-your-5k-pr/ (Accessed 16 Mar 2024)

Stryd; Training Plans
Training with Stryd
Available at: https://help.stryd.com/en/collections/3802281-training-with-stryd (Accessed 16 Mar 2024)

Stryd; Workout app
>Workout app
>Available at: https://help.stryd.com/en/articles/6879318-how-to-do-a-structured-workout (Accessed 16 Mar 2024)

Suunto; Watch
>Suunto Sport Watch Collection
>Available at: https://www.suunto.com/en-gb/Product-search/See-all-Sports-Watches/ (Accessed 16 Mar 2024)

Today's Plan
>Today's Plan
>Available at: https://www.todaysplan.com.au/ (Accessed 16 Mar 2024)

TrainingPeaks
>TrainingPeaks
>Available at: https://www.trainingpeaks.com/ (Accessed 16 Mar 2024)

TrainingPeaks: Mobile App
>TrainingPeaks Mobile App
>Available at: https://www.trainingpeaks.com/learn/articles/trainingpeaks-mobile-home-view/ (Accessed 16 Mar 2024)

TrainingPeaks; Coach Search
TrainingPeaks Coach Search
Available at:
https://www.trainingpeaks.com/coaches/search (Accessed 16 Mar 2024)

TrainingPeaks; Premium
TrainingPeaks Premium
Available at:
https://www.trainingpeaks.com/pricing/for-athletes/ (Accessed 16 Mar 2024)

TrainingPeaks; Sync Your Garmin and TrainingPeaks Accounts
TrainingPeaks Sync Your Garmin and TrainingPeaks Accounts
Available at:
https://www.trainingpeaks.com/account/garminconnect (Accessed 16 Mar 2024)

TrainingPeaks; Training Plans
TrainingPeaks Running Training Plans
Available at:
https://www.trainingpeaks.com/training-plans/running/?language=en&sort.field=soldCount&sort.dir=desc&keyword=power&index=0 (Accessed 16 Mar 2024)

TrainingPeaks; Training platform
Training platform
Available at: https://app.trainingpeaks.com (Accessed 16 Mar 2024)

Van Dijk and Van Megen; The Power-Time Relationship

Van Dijk, H. & Van Megen, R. (2017) The Secret of Running (pp 98-106). Maidenhead: Meyer & Meyer Sport (UK) Ltd

Watchletic

Watchletic
Available at: https://www.watchletic.com/ (Accessed 16 Mar 2024)

Wikipedia; Peter Riegel

Peter Riegel
Available at:
https://en.wikipedia.org/wiki/Peter_Riegel
(Accessed 16 Mar 2024)

Wikipedia; Power (Physics)

Power (Physics)
Available at:
https://en.wikipedia.org/wiki/Power_(physics) (Accessed 16 Mar 2024)

Wikipedia; Steady State (Biochemistry)

Steady State (Biochemistry)
Available at:
https://en.wikipedia.org/wiki/Steady_state_(biochemistry) (Accessed 16 Mar 2024)

Wikipedia; VO2 max

VO2 max
Available at:
https://en.wikipedia.org/wiki/VO2_max
(Accessed 16 Mar 2024)

WKO
>WKO5
>Available at:
><https://www.trainingpeaks.com/wko5/>
>(Accessed 16 Mar 2024)

WKO; Managing Athletes
>WKO Managing Athletes in WKO
>Available at:
><https://www.wko5.com/athlete-management> (Accessed 16 Mar 2024)

Afterwords

Is this book a handy reference? Was it an interesting read?

I hope you've learned something about Running with Power, and I'd like to hear from you.

You can email me at **from1runner2another** at **gmail.com**. Even better, post your question in the [f1r2a; Facebook Group], and I'll do my best to answer it. That way, others will benefit from the conversation.

I'd like to thank my wife, Jane, for her editorial advice. As a non-runner, her feedback was critical in ensuring that this book explained things simply and clearly.

I'd also like to thank the following people who gave me open and honest feedback on drafts of this book, and without whose thoughts, opinions, and suggestions for improvement, I would most likely have included far too much detail and way too many complex (and unnecessary) explanations: Andy Dubois, James Brereton, Alistair Brereton-Halls, Ewan Cameron.

Finally, a very special thank you to Steve Palladino, an expert in Running with Power, who provided invaluable corrections and additions. Steve, I know how precious your time is, and I am incredibly grateful you were able to spare some time for me. Thanks!

If you purchased this book online, I would be grateful if you could post a review on the site where you made your purchase. These reviews are essential for self-published authors, and it's sad but true that readers seldom bother to post their comments, good or bad. If you have any suggestions about improving this book, please include them in your review – I read them all.

Thank you!

Steve Bateman, February 2024

About the Author

I'm a runner who started running at 50 to keep fit for squash. My squash-playing days are over, but my running is still going strong.

I'm a member of the Lonely Goat Running Club – independent from any local UK running clubs.

from1runner2another is a Facebook group to share learning and best practices with others (sharing **from one runner to another**). It's also a place to share running journeys as we improve (changing **from one runner to another**).

I enjoyed sharing and learning from others so much that I decided to certify as a running coach.

After a COVID-enforced delay, I certified as an England Athletics Coach in Running Fitness (CiRF) and from1runner2another opened for business. I coach using UK Coaching's Code of Practice for Sports Coaches.

I firmly believe there's a runner in all of us (no matter how old), and that anyone can start running or continue to improve while minimising injury risk and having fun.

And I believe that Running with Power is the most effective way to train.

Printed in Great Britain
by Amazon